ESSENTIAL
MILITARY JEEP

ESSENTIAL
MILITARY JEEP

WILLYS, FORD & BANTAM MODELS 1941-45

GRAHAM SCOTT

MOTORBOOKS
INTERNATIONAL

This edition first published in 1996 by Bay View Books Limited, Bideford, Devon, EX39 2PZ England

© MBI Publishing Company

Published by Motorbooks International, an imprint of MBI Publishing Company, Galtier Plaza, Suite 200, 380 Jackson Street, St. Paul, MN 55101-3885 USA

The information in this book is true and complete to the best of our knowledge. All recommendations are made without any guarantee on the part of the author or Publisher, who also disclaim any liability incurred in connection with the use of this data or specific details.

We recognize that some words, model names and designations, for example, mentioned herein are the property of the trademark holder. We use them for identification purposes only. This is not an official publication.

Motorbooks International titles are also available at discounts in bulk quantity for industrial or sales-promotional use. For details write to Special Sales Manager at Motorbooks International Wholesalers & Distributors, Galtier Plaza, Suite 200, 380 Jackson Street, St. Paul, MN 55101-3885 USA.

Library of Congress Cataloging-in-Publication Data Available
ISBN 1 870979 76 1

Edited by Mark Hughes
Typesetting and design by Chris Fayers & Sarah Ward
Printed in China

CONTENTS

THE ERA BEFORE JEEP

Converted Ford Model T could have the Vickers machine gun in the front or the back, and carried four men. It lacked power and four-wheel drive but was in use 25 years before the Jeep.

The Jeep has been a vehicle of war and peace, so it seems fitting that its ancestry can be traced back to both. The Jeep is so right, so obviously correct in both theory and practice, that it seems too obvious, clearly the only answer. But that is hindsight. For about 40 years before its appearance manufacturers and military planners grappled with the problem of making a light vehicle that could cross country while carrying men and supplies.

It must be said at once that the Jeep is not simply a logical progression of those 40 years. It was a giant leap, a breakthrough of breathtaking simplicity at exactly the right moment. Certainly, what went before affected it, if only because the planners knew what did not work, but the Jeep was a huge step forward. At once it rendered all existing vehicles obsolete, and automotive design departments world-wide must have been filled with the sound of foreheads being slapped with palms of hands.

That is not to say that there was not an amazing amount of thought and smart ideas around before 1940, just that they never quite worked. To actually say when

Even before World War II, the Germans tended towards more complex, high-quality machinery. This is an inter-war troop carrier designed by the Austrian company, Steyr-Daimler-Puch.

our story begins is like asking when weapons started, but there had been efforts to get men moved around without tiring out the horses ever since the engine was invented. Military manoeuvres in France in the late 1890s were accompanied by two-, three- and four-wheeled vehicles, and over the ensuing decades four-wheeled then four-wheel drive vehicles were converted from civilian motors for reconnaissance and liaison duties in Europe.

As the first decade of the 20th Century started to accelerate, military authorities dabbled with motorised transport, but it was, inevitably, World War I that cranked up everyone's effort. Before that, in 1904, the French had fitted a Hotchkiss machine gun to a Panhard, a combination that proved successful in scouting hostile territory in Morocco, but the spotlight then passed to the USA as the builder of mass-produced vehicles. Wars use up a lot of vehicles.

Cadillac produced big V8 staff cars and ambulances from 1910, but Ford provided the lion's share with its Model T. This served as scout car, liaison vehicle, ambulance and everything else that could be demanded of it. The British used the Model T in Mesopotamia and Egypt, where, fitted with a Vickers machine gun, it gave a good account of itself in the desert. It was light (indeed it could be stripped down to just 1200lb), it could take a machine gun and four men, and it could cope with rough tracks – all this a quarter of a century before the Jeep. The Model T was close but not close enough. The engine gave a mere 20bhp, only the rear wheels were driven and the body was made of wood, but the majority of the American Expeditionary Force must still have wished for one instead of the feet belonging either to themselves, a horse or a mule.

Equally, the lucky men were transported in trucks made by either the FWD Auto Company or by the

Thomas B Jeffery Company. The former made three- and five-ton trucks which worked so well that the British Government ordered 400 for its own troops and supplies, while the Americans also made good use of these four-wheel drive trucks. The FWDs also proved themselves in 1916 in Mexico, when Pancho Villa came up against Lieutenant George Patton. The Jeffery Quadruple Drive Truck (or 'Quad') was similarly successful, with nearly 11,500 produced in the last year of World War I. This was an advanced one-and-a-half ton truck with four-wheel steering, drive and braking, which is pretty impressive for a mass-produced military vehicle. Powered by a 36bhp four-cylinder engine, it served American, British and French forces throughout the war with some distinction, although production dropped off sharply at the end of hostilities.

At the end of World War I there was the usual slow decline of both interest and budget for mechanising the infantry, but four bitter years of war had not been entirely lost on the planners. Larger trucks sank in soft going, and were generally big enough to attract unwelcome attention from enemy gunners. What was needed was something small that could still carry men and material. What was available was a selection of civilian cars and trucks.

Despite the knowledge that size really did matter, and the less of it the better, several designs were based on trucks or even tractors. Various companies tried all the options. The Belgian Type 47 light tractor had two engines, front and back, but never made it into production. The American Minneapolis-Moline company spent the late 1930s converting heavy tractors to pull artillery and to carry light machine guns with slightly more success (and claimed that its vehicle was the first to be called a Jeep).

The Germans, predictably, went a slightly more complex route. Vidal und Sohn of Hamburg produced a

Marmon-Herrington had plenty of ideas on different types of vehicles. This 1930s doorless half-tonner had **selectable four-wheel drive and was big enough to carry men or material – in this case a motorbike.**

Tempo G1200 that had a pair of two-cylinder engines, again front and back, while the Mercedes-Benz G5 152 had both four-wheel drive and four-wheel steering in a high-class package that must have had a phenomenal unit cost. It remained in production until the Germans were fighting World War II.

All these vehicles were designed for a multitude of purposes and, obviously, light cross-country runs were not one of the major criteria. The Americans were also suffering under the same budgetary constraints that meant that nothing could be built from a clean sheet of paper. During the 1920s this was accepted grudgingly, so a programme of 'Cross-Country Cars' was instigated to convert road cars like the Ford Model T and Series K

Italy tended to convert existing vehicles to military use, a practice followed by many nations with small **budgets. This is a Fiat 1014 of 1929, showing good ramp breakover angles with its short wheelbase.**

Russian GAZ-61-40, of 1939. Under that lengthy bonnet ran a 3.5-litre straight-six engine, giving an impressive 85bhp. Cross-country performance was good, and it led on to conversions as open-topped tractors for pulling anti-tank artillery.

The GAZ-61 followed rapidly on from the 61-40, but it stood 75in high, making it a comfortable but easy target. By 1941 the officers were in Russian Jeeps (Ivan-Willys), which meant less comfort but also less of a sitting target.

Chevrolet. Despite a lot of work, the inclusion of machine guns, ammunition and other tools pushed the weight up too far, with detrimental effects on handling and the ability to avoid sinking into the nearest bog. The tests proved four-wheel drive was superior to any other system, but the whole programme folded in 1932 with no breakthrough vehicle in sight.

The light truck route was more successfully followed by the Marmon-Herrington Company as the final years before World War II started to run out. The company's bigger 4x4 trucks worked well but were simply too large for forward duties. However, the Ford-based half-ton truck had four-wheel drive, a low silhouette and a top speed of over 35mph. The American Army liked this

truck enough to order 64 of them in 1939, although nicknaming it 'The Darling' did seem to carry that liking rather too far.

Marmon-Herrington further modified the half-ton chassis with a four-seater doorless body, which became the Command Car. By the time it went into production in 1939 the Ford chassis had been replaced by a Dodge one. The Dodge Command Car did solid work during the war, as did the offshoot Dodge Weapons Carrier. Dodge and Marmon-Herrington vehicles featured selectable four-wheel drive, so that on-road performance could be hustled along in two-wheel drive, with four-wheel drive being selected by the driver before going off-road. This had huge implications for the speed with

Two views of the Russian GAZ-67B, the successor to the earlier Russian vehicles seen here. It was produced from 1943 until the 1950s and shows the clear influence of the Jeep, which had arrived with the Soviets two years earlier.

which troops and supplies could be shifted between locations or battlefields. Nevertheless, it was accepted that all these vehicles were simply too large and high for the role of reconnaissance across country.

Countries like Italy simply converted small road cars like the Fiat Balilla to military specification and then called the result a Spider 508 Militare. Things like axle ratios were lowered and a four-speed gearbox put in, but the result was hardly ground-breaking. More innovative were the Russians: in the 1930s Russia was going the way of three axles to help with cross-country performance but an engineer at the main GAZ plant, Vitaly Grachev, bravely promoted four-wheel drive. Bear in mind that Stalin was executing people, in or out of uniform, in their millions. Anything could count as sabotage against the Army, so when Grachev pushed to have production of the triple-axle GAZ-21 command car

halted, to be replaced by a four-wheel drive vehicle, he was quite literally putting his neck on the line.

Fortunately for him, his faith was vindicated and the GAZ-61 went into production. It was based on American technical input from Marmon-Herrington but with plenty of trips to the GAZ parts bin. The first command car, designated the GAZ-61-40, had a cabriolet body with a six-cylinder engine, while a GAZ-61 sedan soon followed. Both vehicles had excellent off-road abilities with fine approach and departure angles, as well as breakover angles. Generals like Zhukov and Timoshenko used them until they were discontinued in 1941, when Russian production went over to machines

The British Army used the Austin Seven, although it was too light to mount heavy weapons. In various guises it was built as a military reconnaissance vehicle around the world, from Japan to America. The silhouette of the aptly-named 'Belly Flopper' of 1937 (left) was only 33in high. Two soldiers lying prone could be transported, but poor ground clearance and ride quality meant this strange prototype based on an Austin Seven remained a one-off.

based on yet another American design – the Jeep.

These huge Russian machines worked well, but they were particularly tall. A low silhouette was acknowledged to be a vital requirement for troops wishing to keep their heads not just down but on. But following this idea to its logical conclusion showed that logic sometimes gets a bit fuzzy. The logic ran that the best way of stopping soldiers from having to sit too high was to get them to lie down.

In 1937 the American Army tested what was described as 'a snake in the grass'. Lying just over 33in off the ground at its highest point, the device could take two men lying down and scoot them about at up to 30mph. It could also take a .30-cal machine gun and 1500 rounds

of ammunition, but it had no bodywork to offer protection and, even more importantly, no suspension. Designed by Master Sergeant Melvyn C. Wiley, who was working on earlier ideas of Captain Robert G. Howie, the machine was shown to the Army, who sank the idea by judging that ride quality and ground clearance were insufficient. It was a novel solution, but with suspension coming only from the tyres the ride quality can best be imagined by remembering what it is like to lie on a toboggan hurtling over rough ground. How you could then steer, by means of levers, and fire a machine gun at the same time is best not dwelt upon. The name of 'Belly Flopper' was well earned.

Also used by the British Army was the Morris Minor, seen here radio-equipped during manoeuvres at Saarbrucken in 1935.

The Beaverette 1 was built on a Standard chassis with metal plate backed by oak boards for armour protection. Firepower amounted to one Bren gun. This heavy, unwieldy two-wheel drive vehicle looks like it comes from soon after the end of World War I, but this photo was taken in Britain in 1940, just after the Germans had forced the evacuation at Dunkirk.

Perhaps the most relevant idea to come out of the Belly Flopper was its use of a converted American Austin chassis with power fed to the front wheels from a rear-mounted engine, which was a converted Austin Seven four-cylinder. For such a small machine, the British Austin Seven was to have a disproportionately large impact on military designs during the 1930s in countries as far apart as the USA and Japan.

This lightweight road car was first produced in Britain in 1922 as a low-priced vehicle for every family – the Mini would aim for much the same market decades later. The Seven sold in huge numbers, and was soon taken up by the military as a light and reliable vehicle for carrying men, equipment, radio links and all the other duties of a military all-rounder. It was not terribly good off-road but could be manhandled about when the going got rough. So suitable was it as a basis for all manner of military conversions that it was made under licence in Japan. Similarly, if more surprisingly, it was also built under licence by BMW in Germany in the 1930s. Significantly, the German *Reichswehr* used it as a training vehicle for its motorised units. But it was not seen as a front-line machine by them, as it was by many other nations.

Motoring tastes on the other side of the Atlantic from Britain were very different, notably in that Americans did not really take to small-car motoring. Nevertheless, the American Austin Car Company started producing Austin Seven-based vehicles in 1929 at a reasonable price. Five years later the company was bankrupt as sales plummeted, leaving the way clear for a cheap take-over by Roy Evans, who formed the American Bantam Car Company

from the wreckage. By 1938 the Pennsylvania National Guard was trying out three Bantams with such good results that the Quartermaster Corps started to take an official interest in the idea of a modified vehicle as a reconnaissance car. If the Bantam was ever to grow to maturity the company needed to find a new market, and soon – by mid-1940 the company was heading into terminal decline, with just 15 employees.

The Austin's main competitor in the cheap car stakes had been the Willys 77, produced by the Willys-Overland Company. This too was a company in some difficulties by 1940, although its state was not as parlous as that of Bantam. A bewildering and aggressive series of take-overs and stock manoeuvrings set against the problems of the Great Depression had sent the company on a roller-coaster of boom and bust. One outcome was the fatal heart attack suffered by founder John North Willys in 1935, another was the arrival of two men, Delmar 'Barney' Roos as Vice President and Chief Engineer in 1938 and Joseph Frazer as President a year later. While Frazer explored every sales avenue going, Roos redesigned the four-cylinder 134.2cu in engine that had been in use since 1926. He upped power from 49bhp at 3200rpm to 63bhp at 3800rpm and made it stronger and easier to drive.

Willys-Overland now had massive assets in terms of buildings and floor space, and a memory of greatness gone. It had a fine engine and some good vehicles but it needed more to really expand, if not survive.

The year 1940 was to prove the catalyst for both Willys-Overland and Bantam.

BATTLE FOR THE CONTRACT

On 27 June 1940, while Spitfires and Messerschmitts were dogfighting over the English Channel, the American Quartermaster Corps Ordnance Technical Committee released specifications for a new military vehicle. The requirements were strict:

1) Four-wheel drive
2) Minimum speed 3mph
3) Empty weight 1300lb
4) Payload 600lb
5) Wheelbase 80in
6) Height 36in
7) Track 47in
8) Ground clearance 6.5in

How it all began. The first Bantam outside the factory with, far left, Karl Probst looking exhausted and, in the driving seat, Harold Crist.

Those specifications were tough enough but the clincher was the deadline – 22 July at 9.00am. Not even a month away…

Everything had moved at remarkable speed up to this date since a technical committee within the Army had been working on draft requirements only since the beginning of June. This had been prompted by the viewing of three Bantam vehicles, which did not come up to expectations but which interested the Army enough to take it a stage further – with a war already

The Bantam's rounded front end did not survive the first revision, but the Spicer-supplied front axle had a longer life.

Just a little bit of body roll is displayed by the Bantam in an early test run with four aboard round the factory.

bursting the other side of the Atlantic you can see why things started to accelerate. Three military engineers, Bill Burgan, Bob Brown and W. Beasley, were joined by Major Howie, who was the father of the 'Belly Flopper' device that the Army had previously rejected. These four men worked on the specification for the quarter-ton truck that eventually led to the release of the requirements on 27 June.

Over 135 companies were asked to submit plans by 22 July, and follow up with 70 finished prototypes available within 75 days. Eight of these prototypes had to have four-wheel steering. An initial prototype had to be ready in just 49 days, with the rest following within the next 26 days. For many companies this was simply impossible – the parameters were so tight that no existing vehicle could be converted. The requirements demanded

A Bantam chassis at the factory manages to weight-lift a load more than six times its specified 500lb rating.

that a company start with a clean sheet of paper and come up in less than a month with a brand new design that could be translated into metal just a few weeks later. No wonder that only two of the 135 companies even replied to the invitation. This was going to be an exclusive party, at least to start with, before the gate-crashers arrived.

It is now ten days before the plans have to be presented. It is night, but a 1938 Buick Coupe is driving hard through the darkness. It is on the roads between Detroit and Butler, Pennsylvania, and the driver is in a hurry. It is a journey not without its dangers. Behind the wheel is Karl Probst, a 56-year-old motor engineer who runs a small independent engineering firm in Detroit. Ill health when he was younger has slowed down a promising career with larger automotive design companies, but his inventiveness remains.

Probst has, this very day, been told about the requirements for a new design but he is not sure that it can be done because it means so much, so new, so fast. He has been resisting calls to help at Bantam but a series of heavyweight 'phone calls from people like William Knudsen, head of the National Defense Advisory Commission, and Frank Fenn, head of Bantam, have made him change his mind. In essence, they have been telling him that he has to help, to help America. Money?

If they do not get the contract he does not get paid. Normally he might have refused but the news is full of Europe falling to the Germans, of Dunkirk and of little England standing on its own, taking on the might of the *Wehrmacht*, U-boats and *Luftwaffe*. Bantam, too, is a small company, teetering on the edge of extinction and Karl Probst's patriotic soul is stirred. He drives on through the night.

Probst arrives safely in Butler, stopping only once, in Toledo, where he speaks with Bob Lewis of the Spicer transmission company. By Wednesday lunchtime, 22 June, he is seated at a drafting table at the beginning of a marathon session with pen and paper. He works 18 hours, sleeps for eight hours, then works another 18 hours. By the end of Friday he has designed the Jeep.

So it was that Probst had a complete set of blueprints ready for the moment when bidding opened at Camp Holabird at 9.00am on 22 July. Also present at this important meeting were representatives from Ford, Crosley and Willys-Overland, but of these only Willys-Overland submitted a bid. Although the Willys-Overland proposal was in a rough and unready state, it was a cheaper bid – but this advantage was countered by the company's desire to extend the time for the first prototype by a further 45 days. Unsurprisingly, the contract, worth $171,185, went to Bantam. Although it

Early testing of the Bantam by the military at Camp Holabird showed up a few weaknesses, but the overall verdict was overwhelmingly positive. One of the testers, Major Herbert Lawes, said "I believe this unit will make history".

took until 5 August for this decision to be announced officially, Bantam was told only half an hour after bidding closed that it had the contract. Everything looked rosy for them.

So, a small company, struggling on the edge of extinction, takes on the big boys, clearly puts in a better and more professional design, and is rewarded with a contract that should be the start of its climb back from the brink. It sounds like a fairy tale, does it not? The trouble is, reality is no fairy tale.

One little problem was of Bantam's own making. Probst decided as soon as he saw the original brief that a weight of 1300lb was unrealistic. He knew he could not achieve it and he was certain nobody else could either, so he simply ignored it. As a result, his original design weighed in around 600lb over the limit. Bantam's military sales representative, retired Navy Commander Charles Payne, simply wrote '1273lb' where the bid forms asked for the dry weight of the design. How this would affect things would have to wait until the first prototype was actually built and being assessed by the military.

That first prototype was hand-built in a hurry. The delivery date for its initial trial was 23 September, and it

was finished on 21 September. Naturally time did not allow a whole vehicle to be built up from scratch, so a great deal had to come from various parts bins. The basis was the Bantam roadster that the military had already tried and discarded. It had a beefed-up frame holding a more powerful Continental four-cylinder engine. The Bantam unit previously in place gave only 20bhp, but the Continental engine managed 46bhp at 3250rpm with a healthy 86lb ft of torque at 1800rpm. Power went through a Warner Gears primary gearbox, with three forward gears and one reverse. Sucking through a single-barrel Stromberg carburettor, the engine ran on a six-volt battery and seemed powerful enough, assuming it was not asked to haul too much weight.

The frame was channel-section steel, stouter than on the roadster, with four cross members. On this frame went the doorless steel bodywork, with sturdy bumpers, exposed wheels and functional wings that on this first model were curved rather than flat. It looked remarkably like the Jeep we know and love, although it had a rather more rounded front end.

Underneath the bodywork Probst and his newly expanded team of engineers fitted kit from all over the place. When he broke his journey to Butler by stopping

BATTLE FOR THE CONTRACT

Willys made two Quads, after clearly studying the early Bantam entry. It was the more powerful

Go-Devil engine under that similarly rounded bonnet that helped win the day.

Bantam eventually made over 1100 of the BRC-40,

complete with the front end inspired by Ford.

off at Spicer he certainly did not waste his time. Spicer was just about the only company that, off the shelf, could supply the axles necessary. Modified versions of those found on the Studebaker Champion car, these fully floating units had a 4.88:1 ratio and were joined by a Spicer transfer case which allowed for the shift from two- to four-wheel drive.

Suspension was semi-elliptical springs with Gabriel telescopic shock absorbers, controlling the movement of the 4×16in five-bolt steel wheels. Braking on all four wheels was by 9in drums. Add a fold-down windscreen and a canvas hood and there you have what would become the BRC-40, which stands for Bantam Reconnaissance Command – 40 horsepower. The vehicle was little more than an assembly of components made by companies other than Bantam yet, somehow, the result was more than the sum of its parts.

Weight was well over target but otherwise most

figures stacked up. Ground clearance had been specified as 6.5in, but it was 9in. The wheelbase of 79.5in was virtually the 80in specified, and most other dimensions were correct although the height was a little more than demanded – due partly to the increased ground clearance.

Bantam now had a finished vehicle that roughly conformed to the stringent specifications. Nobody else in America had even come close to the design or the time scale. Now it was time to put the vehicle to the test, in the full knowledge that the company's future hung in the balance. Camp Holabird, about 200 miles away from the Bantam factory, was the site of the proposed testing as it was a well-specified proving ground with all the natural and man-made obstacles necessary to push any vehicle to destruction. The Bantam had to be there by 5.00pm on 23 September. Probst and plant manager Harold Crist got in, fired it up and set off, effectively running the vehicle in on the way. They arrived with just half an hour to spare. The single prototype had now done 400 miles, and ahead of it lay over 3000 miles of punishing driving at the hands of a professional crew of military vehicle testers, who would be pushing it until it broke.

Major Herbert Lawes, who had driven just about every military vehicle in existence, was the first military driver to test the Jeep. Before he took the wheel he asked Crist to drive the vehicle up a 60% slope in second gear – Crist complied with no problem. Major Lawes then set out on a 15min thrash over some of the toughest terrain in the area. He returned saying, "I believe this unit will make history".

Of course, it was not as simple as that, as the prototype had to be tested over the next three weeks. If anything is to be Army-proof it must be able to withstand the most clumsy and brutal treatment, so the testing was deliberately hard – but at least there was no wind-tunnel testing. The exercise included driving off a platform 4ft in the air at 30mph, and endless full-bore runs down logging trails with tree trunks set into the ground at irregular intervals. After 20 days the frame side-members finally cracked under the strain, but by then it was obvious to everyone that the Bantam had proved itself well up to the job.

Not that it was perfect. Twenty weaknesses were found, and it was felt that the weight was excessive and the power output insufficient. The weight was a ticklish problem, of course, because it was well over the specified limit. However, practicality prevailed when a large cavalry officer managed to lift the rear end of the Bantam off the ground unaided. The thinking went that if two men could lift a Bantam it was not too heavy after all.

After receiving praise that went as far as describing the Bantam as the best vehicle ever tested at Holabird, the team went back to the factory to begin building the rest of the 70 prototypes demanded by the original tender. Before these had been finished the military were keen enough to place an order for a further 1500 vehicles to be built by Bantam. This should have been a moment for Bantam to savour, coming as it did at a time when the factory had been virtually shut down. But this is business, not a fairy tale.

Ford and Willys observers at the Camp Holabird trials had been making notes as fast as their pens could write. In the event this was wasted effort. With the testing handed over to the Army, the Bantam design then belonged to the military, and they simply copied the unique blueprints and gave copies to both Ford and Willys. One could question the ethics of such a move, but they represented a real concern that Bantam simply was not big enough to produce so many vehicles. And everyone knew that the numbers needed would be colossal if America went to war...

As soon as the blueprints got into the hands of the rivals, they set off back to their factories and subjected them to close scrutiny. Both companies then said they wanted to produce prototypes, and at their own expense. Before these were even ready the Quartermaster Corps was pushing for the 1500-unit order, placed at Bantam, to be split between the three companies. Bantam fought back hard, pointing out that it had been the only company to come up with a plan on time and the only one to produce a working prototype. Henry Stimson, Secretary of War, accepted the argument and the whole order remained at Bantam, but it was obvious that too many people did not have enough confidence in Bantam's production capabilities.

By November 1940 Ford and Willys had each produced a working prototype, and both were at Camp Holabird for testing. The Willys Quad arrived on 11 November, 12 days before the Ford Pygmy. At stake was an order for a further 1500 vehicles for each company if the prototypes fulfilled the Army's specifications. From the outset neither of them did since the designers, like Probst at Bantam, had reached the conclusion that the weight limit was simply unattainable.

Given that the Bantam blueprints had been the basis for both the Ford and Willys vehicles, it was no surprise that they looked remarkably like the Bantam. The main visual difference was that Ford went for a flat grille front, whereas Willys copied the Bantam's more rounded grille. Bantam observers at these trials must have been fuming as

Excellent shot showing the military testing two contenders back-to-back. In the foreground is the Ford GP with, behind it, the Willys MA, complete with logo stamped into the front of the bonnet.

they saw all their earlier work, their lead on the others, simply evaporate away.

At the time, neither Ford nor Willys was complacent since both their prototypes suffered problems when tested hard. Ford had not been particularly keen to be involved with the project at first because it was concentrating on improving its road cars, but the company soon came to see the benefits, and pressure was also added by the military because it was obvious that Ford had the largest production capacity of anyone. Given the time scale, the Ford Pygmy was not a bad effort but, like Bantam and Willys, the company had been forced to use existing components as a basis for the machine.

With most of Ford's efforts going on big road cars, the only four-cylinder engine the company had available

was from the Ferguson Dearborn tractor. This was far from ideal: tractor engines are designed to run for long periods at steady speeds, but soldiers thrash military vehicles up and down the rev range the whole time. Power output of 45bhp at 3600rpm was reasonable, but this engine simply could not stand up to the sort of use demanded. To make matters worse, there was only one transmission to go with this engine. With three forward speeds from the old Model A gearbox and no synchromesh, this transmission was hopelessly out of date. The Ford powertrain was not a good combination.

Willys, on the other hand, had the finest engine of the lot. The four-cylinder that 'Barney' Roos had tweaked for the Willys Whippet in 1938 gave the best, most reliable power of any of the three units on offer. Dubbed the Go-Devil, this engine was much admired by the military testers since it was also comfortably the most powerful, at 63bhp.

By this time the military planners had accepted that their weight target was unrealistic, so it was raised from

The Ford GP was better than the Pygmy and inspired the front end styling for the Willys MB and Ford GPW.

Ford GP interior (below left), which did not survive. Note the handbrake cluttering up the area already crowded by transmission levers. The Ford engine (below) was not in the same league as the powerful Willys Go-Devil.

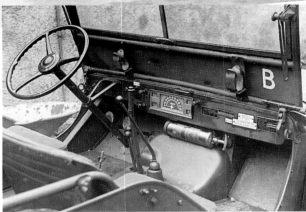

1300lb to 2160lb. This let Bantam off the hook, plus its prototype had the best fuel consumption of the three. Braking and steering were also felt to be superior on the Bantam. Against that, the Ford was the most comfortable, and the easiest to use. Importantly, it was also liked for its flat bonnet since it was felt that this would give a useful surface. The rounded bonnets of the Bantam and Willys were considered less practical.

Despite having the best engine by some margin, the Willys could not come in under the revised weight limit. At 2423lb it was the heaviest, compared to the Bantam's 2050lb and the Ford's 2150lb. Surprisingly, Willys still received an order for 1500 vehicles but it was made clear that the weight problem would have to be addressed, and addressed quickly.

Ahead lay the Service Finals test where the three companies would compete to win the battle of the 'US Tentative Specifications USA-LP-997A'. Huge orders were in the offing, but to reach the goal the contestants would have to meet some stringent criteria:

1) A maximum level road speed of at least 55mph, at a point in the rev range that was not over peak horsepower.
2) A minimum level road speed of 3mph.
3) At that 3mph the vehicle had to be able to ford water 18in deep.
4) The ability to operate with tyre chains fitted.
5) Approach and departure angles had to be 45 and 35 degrees respectively.

It was clear that the Willys had the potential to win, but not at the current weight. The obvious weight-loss route would be to put a lighter engine under the bonnet, but everyone knew that the Go-Devil unit was the main attraction. There was no other way for it: Willys was going to have to go through the whole vehicle to pare away the pounds. About 12% of the vehicle's weight needed to go.

Replacing the heavy carbon steel frame with an alloy one saved 115lb, and the body itself lost another 35lb.

Testing in 1942 with the Ford GP – called the Peep at the time – in wilder parts of Britain. Lt Col Gardner in North Wales (above), and vehicles complete with snow chains to aid mud traction (right) on Skiddaw in the Lake District. The lack of weather protection is obvious from the expressions...

The Ford-designed two-part windscreen was adapted, taking off 14lb, while 18lb came off with a new seat design. Every single bolt, washer and cotter pin was evaluated and many were downsized. Even so, the vehicle now known as the Willys MA was perilously close to being overweight. The final cut was the reduction of the paint thickness to one coat. This lost 9lb and finally the Jeep was under the weight restriction. Willys was ready for the final test.

After back-to-back testing of the three vehicles, it was obvious that the Willys was the best option. It was more powerful and, thanks to having been based on the inspired original Bantam design, it was practical and simply 'right'. The Bantam could not match the power and had simply lost its lead. Additionally, testing showed that the Bantam overheated and the transmission was prone to breakage and rapid wear. It had too many 'bugs'. The Ford engine was basically a tractor unit with the governor taken off and, without it, the engine soon ran its bearings and caused more problems.

At stake was an order for 16,000 units, a prize that both Bantam and Willys needed and Ford would find easy to deliver. Although the Willys design was the most competent, this apparently was not obvious to everyone. The Quartermaster Corps was still championing Ford, presumably because of its larger production potential. For a while it looked as though the Ford Pygmy with a tractor-based engine was going to beat the other two, even though in the exhaustive trials it had come last. Fortunately, the War Production Office was headed by William Knudsen, a man with a mission.

Of Danish extraction, he had already seen his native country attacked and occupied by the Germans, and he was only too aware of what was coming. He refused to countenance anything that would stand in the way of the practical execution of war preparation. Ford protested vigorously but it already had enormous labour problems and the last thing the programme needed was a strike. The award was sensibly given to Willys. On 23 July 1941 the Quartermaster Corps agreed a contract for Willys to

Bantam BRC-40 in full fighting guise, complete with complex machine gun mounts and extra **stowage bin. This example was in action with the British 6th Armoured Division.**

One of nearly 4500 Ford GPs built, in use with the British airborne troops. **Note the steering wheel cut down to fit inside an aircraft.**

supply 16,000 revised units, the Willys MB, at a unit price of $739.

Ford may have lost the battle but it certainly had not lost the war. It was uneasily decided that there simply could not be too many production facilities and, on 10 November 1941, Ford agreed to make the vehicle known as the Jeep. What was so remarkable was that it agreed to make the vehicle to the Willys specifications and plans. This was to be a virtual replica of the vehicles being produced by Willys, right down to the Go-Devil engine. The agreement called for 15,000 units to be produced at a cost of $14,623,900. Willys handed over patents and drawings so that Ford could make the General Purpose Willys (GPW). Willys either made no money or very little money, depending on who you believe, out of this transaction, a deal that could never have occurred without war clouds looming. Less than a month after this agreement the Zeros appeared over Pearl Harbour in Honolulu.

Bantam, unlike Ford, lost out right down the line. More recent analysis shows that Bantam could probably have produced a good number of vehicles, but it had been too widely accepted that Bantam was too small. In the end Bantam made about 2600 BRC-40s, and for the rest of the war it was restricted to making trailers and aircraft landing gear. After the war Bantam went broke and was eventually and ignominiously incorporated into American Rolling Mills in 1956. So much for fairy tales.

JEEP IN DETAIL

The machine produced in such vast numbers during World War II was sketched by one man at Bantam in less than two days. The front end incorporated design ideas, like the flat front grille, from the Ford drawing boards. Under that front end was an engine that had been around since 1926 and that Willys-Overland had breathed on until it was one of the most powerful in its class. Now the vehicle was virtually right, and now it could be made in overwhelming numbers.

But first some rough edges still had to be smoothed off before mass production could begin, and would

Willys and Ford plants all over America poured out the Jeep, making a massive contribution to the war effort. In the end about 650,000 were made.

continue to be worked on as production got under way. The Jeep was really made by just two companies in any volume. The American Bantam Car Company ended up making 2675 Jeeps, being the prototypes and nearly 1200 BRC-40s. Willys-Overland Motors made 1555 Model MA Jeeps and over 360,000 of the mass-production Model MB. And Ford built nearly 4500 of its own

Rear of the chassis, showing the box-section side members and the rear cross members.

The front cross member was tubular on the Willys MB (below left), but of an inverted U section on the Ford GPW (below).

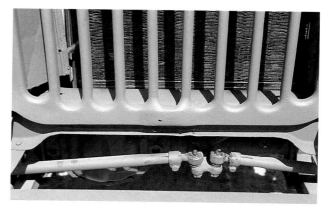

THE JEEP NAME

A whole book could be written just about the derivation of the word Jeep, but it would all be as much speculation to one person as confirmation to another. Certainly there is a fairly strong explanation in the form of the name coming from a contraction of General Purpose (GP), but there are other possibilities. There was a Popeye character in the 1930s called Eugene the Jeep. The Minneapolis-Moline Company, mentioned in the first chapter, used the name for some of its armoured tractors before the war started. A piece in the *Washington Daily News* in February 1941 described the very vehicle. But the only real certainty is that Joseph Frazer, President of Willys-Overland, shrewdly registered the name Jeep as a company trademark.

To minimise vibration damage, the bodywork was isolated from the chassis by shims, at first made from rubber, later from fabric.

Early Willys MB 'slat grill' with the distinctive – and heavy – grille made from welded iron bars.

At first Willys followed the Ford pattern of stamping its name into the body parts (note, under the jerrycan), but stopped this in 1942.

Model GP Jeeps and another 277,896 GPW models (General Purpose Willys, made to the Willys pattern). What was it they made, and how did they differ?

The basic generic Jeep was based on a chassis made by Midland Steel, with two box-section side members running along to kick up over the front and rear wheels. Five cross members then connected the two side members: on Willys versions the front cross member, like the other four, was of tubular cross-section, whereas on the Ford GPW it was of an inverted U shape.

Onto this chassis went the bodywork, in low-carbon steel. The floor was 16-gauge but other panels were of 18-gauge. At first, rubber insulated the body from the frame but, once war restrictions took hold in early 1942, fabric shims were used to separate body and frame at all 16 bolt holes. Both Ford and Willys made their own

**"Run it up th' mountain again, Joe.
It ain't hot enough."**

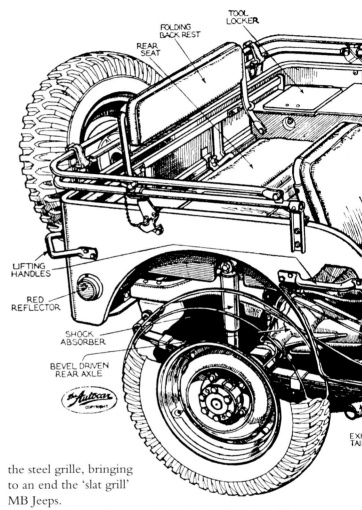

TOOL LOCKER

FOLDING BACK REST

REAR SEAT

LIFTING HANDLES

RED REFLECTOR

SHOCK ABSORBER

BEVEL DRIVEN REAR AXLE

EX TAI

bodies, with Ford using its Lincoln car plant to churn out the GPW bodywork. Prior to that, its GP bodies had been produced by a company called Budd, which had a German subsidiary company that made bodies for the *Wehrmacht* staff cars used by men like Field Marshals Goering and Rommel.

The MB model, produced by Willys and mimicked by Ford, differed from the early MA design most notably at the front end. Gone was the Willys name that had been stamped on the front edge of the bonnet. The bonnet itself was flatter than on the MA while the grille below it now housed the headlamps, which had previously been positioned on the front mudguards. At first the grille was made up of iron bars welded top and bottom. This was an easy unit to make, but it was heavy and prone to breaking if the arc-welding was not up to scratch. All the early vehicles from Bantam, Ford and Willys featured this design, and it was not until Ford produced the GPW that the pressed steel grille appeared. All the Willys MA models had the iron version, as did the first 25,800 MB vehicles. After this the MB also had

the steel grille, bringing to an end the 'slat grill' MB Jeeps.

Behind that grille roared the Go-Devil engine. This had started out in 1926 as the Whippet four-cylinder, a fairly unassuming engine that lacked both horsepower and real reliability. Willys engineer 'Barney' Roos used this as the basis for his engine, enlarging both inlet ports and inlet manifold. A down-draught Carter carburettor was fitted so that the Jeep could keep running on a 20-degree side slope or a 56-degree slope front and rear. Compression ratio was raised from 5.7:1 to 6.48:1 –

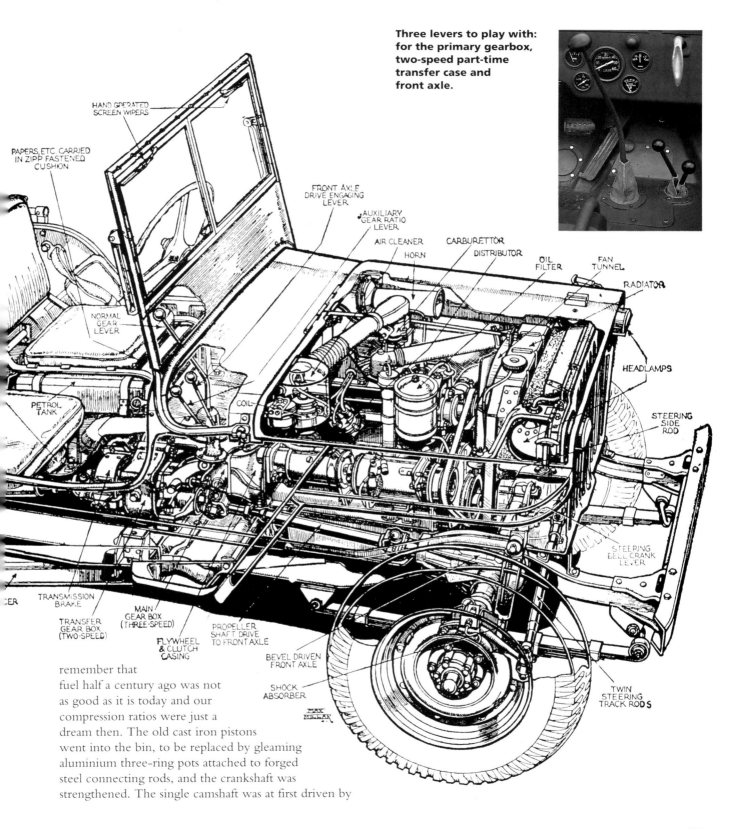

Three levers to play with: for the primary gearbox, two-speed part-time transfer case and front axle.

HAND OPERATED SCREEN WIPERS

PAPERS, ETC. CARRIED IN ZIPP FASTENED CUSHION

FRONT AXLE DRIVE ENGAGING LEVER

AUXILIARY GEAR RATIO LEVER

AIR CLEANER

HORN

CARBURETTOR

DISTRIBUTOR

OIL FILTER

FAN TUNNEL

RADIATOR

NORMAL GEAR LEVER

COIL

HEADLAMPS

PETROL TANK

STEERING SIDE ROD

STEERING BELL CRANK LEVER

TRANSMISSION BRAKE

TRANSFER GEAR BOX (TWO-SPEED)

MAIN GEAR BOX (THREE-SPEED)

FLYWHEEL & CLUTCH CASING

PROPELLER SHAFT DRIVE TO FRONT AXLE

BEVEL DRIVEN FRONT AXLE

SHOCK ABSORBER

TWIN STEERING TRACK RODS

MAX MILLAR

remember that fuel half a century ago was not as good as it is today and our compression ratios were just a dream then. The old cast iron pistons went into the bin, to be replaced by gleaming aluminium three-ring pots attached to forged steel connecting rods, and the crankshaft was strengthened. The single camshaft was at first driven by

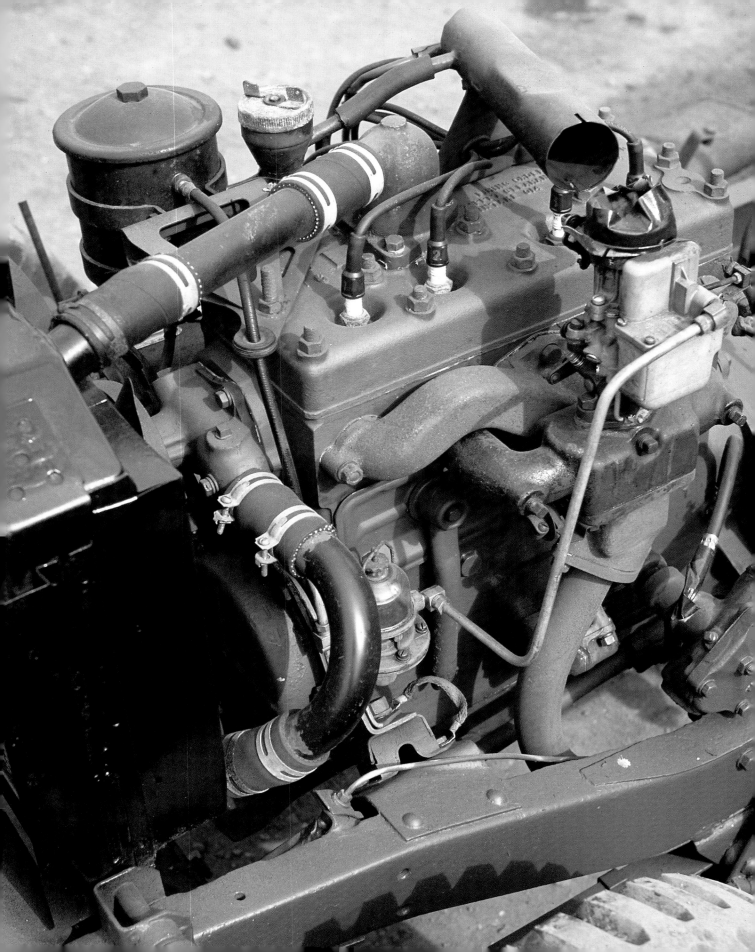

An ingenious touch. Each headlamp was held in place by a single nut which, when loosened, enabled the headlamp to swing up to illuminate the engine bay for night-time maintenance.

chain but, on the later Type 442 engine, this job was taken over by gears. Along with other changes this boosted horsepower on production models from 49bhp to 60bhp at 3600rpm. Maximum torque rose to 105lb ft at just 2000rpm and a governor limited engine speed to 3800rpm, which was a wise move when soldiers were driving. The 134.2cu in (2199cc) engine was a tight fit under the 40in high bonnet but it was worth the squeeze.

Wrapped around this engine was a highly efficient and almost oversized cooling system containing 11 quarts of water – it did not take soldiers in the field long to find

The Willys Go-Devil engine had started life in a small car in 1926 but was one of the strongest, most reliable elements of the war-time Jeep.

this copious source of hot water. The heat source of this washing and shaving water, the four-cylinder unit, fed into a 7.875in Borg & Beck clutch linked to the Model T-84-J transmission made by Warner. This had three forward speeds and one reverse, with synchromesh only on second and third – but drivers at that time were used to having to double declutch to shift cleanly into first gear. Spicer normally supplied the two-speed transfer box, although Brown-Lipe also provided some later on. The 1.97:1 low range was only available when the vehicle was in four-wheel drive, and shifting into low ratio was best attempted at less than walking pace – you had to have the vehicle completely stationary to bring in four-wheel drive.

The two levers for bringing in the front axle drive and the high or low ranges were placed on the floor next to the main gearshift. The gearshift itself moved from the steering column, where it had been on the MA, down to the floor where, the reasoning went, it would be in a more normal position for drivers who had to get used

**Ford production line
churning out GPWs. Note
the arrangement of leaf
springs, shock absorbers**
**and the small drum
brakes – and the tipped-
up headlamp on the
front vehicle.**

to controlling a very wide range of military vehicles.

Running off the engine was a redesigned air cleaner on the MB which conformed with Bureau of Standards regulations. The generator was the 40 amp QMC – Quartermaster Corps – model, again added in the interests of commonality of parts as several trucks already used it. This rationalisation extended to the six-volt electrics and 5in sealed-beam headlamps, along with standard black-out lights front and rear. Autolite, who made the generator, also supplied the starter motor and the voltage regulator.

The engine sat slightly to the left within the chassis, so the suspension had to compensate for the uneven weight distribution. At both ends of the Jeep were semi-elliptic springs made of aluminium alloy. There were eight leaves at the front and nine at the rear, and the left front spring had two heavier-duty leaves to balance up the vehicle. Spring movement was damped by a Bendix shock absorber at each corner, with Bendix also supplying the twin-shoe drum brakes for all four wheels.

Lockheed made the hydraulic system that controlled these drums. At first there was a transmission parking brake but this was soon replaced by a drum brake unit, while the location of the lever that controlled it moved from outside the vehicle next to the driver to inside the vehicle between the seats – that way a passenger stood some chance of getting to it in an emergency.

Inside the Jeep things were as spartan as possible. Seating was for four people with two tubular-framed front seats and a rear bench seat with foldable backrest. The seats were originally filled with 2in foam rubber but, after Pearl Harbour, this was changed to a cattle-hair pad covered in rubber. Given the value of rubber as the war progressed, even this had to go, to be replaced by springs and hair felt. The seat cushions had zips in the bottom so

The front seats were not well designed and led to all manner of ailments if used for a long time.

The only thing worse than the front seats was the back bench seat. Officers hardly ever sat here as it was above the rear axle and something of a pile driver.

that soldiers could stuff a military blanket into the seat to increase the padding, but the zips disappeared in July 1943 as it was found that troops were not using this arrangement. All seating was covered in heavyweight, water-repellent, fire-resistant cotton duck. Given that the occupants for most of the time had as much protection from the elements as a motorcyclist, this material made a lot of sense.

The driver had relatively few controls and gauges. Dials were an ammeter, temperature gauge, speedometer, fuel gauge and oil pressure gauge. The levers for the main transmission, high and low ratios and two- and four-wheel drive were all grouped on the floor on the driver's right side in the middle of the vehicle.

The windscreen had two panes of glass, replacing the single pane of the early prototypes. Ford GPW versions had laminated glass made by a Ford plant, and the oval logo with a manufacturing code was sandblasted on to every screen. This is one example of Ford's obsession with marking every item it contributed to the Jeep. Two

wing nuts held the windscreen to the body, and these could be slackened so that the two-glass shield lay flat on the bonnet, or the whole screen could be removed completely. Because of this facility, the windscreen wipers were operated by hand, to avoid complex and detachable wiring – this was irritating but it worked. Taking off the windscreens also allowed Jeeps to be stacked one on top of another for transportation, the wheels resting on the mudguards of the vehicle below.

Early vehicles had a simple ignition switch in front of the driver which took a standard H-700 key. This was fine until soldiers starting wandering off with the keys and vehicles were suddenly immobilised. The sensible step was taken in December 1942 to fit a handle-type ignition switch that did not need a key. Both Ford and Willys switched at the same time, although the Ford bezels had bumps on them that made them easier to grip for installing or removing.

In the footwell were the three foot pedals for clutch, brake and accelerator, with a footrest beside them. The

The driver obtained all the vital information from five gauges: fuel level, oil pressure, speed, battery power and engine temperature.

Willys clutch and brake pedals were made of stamped steel but Ford used cast iron pedals. The steering wheel, with a horn in the small centre boss, controlled variable-ratio steering made by Ross, just over three turns lock to lock giving a 38ft clockwise turning circle.

Just behind each front seat was a small tool locker, while the petrol tank sat under the seat. Enlarging the tank on the MB to 15 gallons (capacity on the MA was 10 gallons) meant forming it into an L shape and re-routing the exhaust system to exit on the right-hand side. Fuel was on the planners' minds, so another five gallons were carried in a jerrycan, which was attached on the rear of the Jeep.

On the dash was a selection of plates giving vehicle details, instructions on how to operate the transmission systems, and maximum speeds recommended in high and low range. At the far right of the dash was a compartment for storage, although it did not hold much and was not found on the first 20,698 MBs. This should have carried things like the gas mask and eye shields, neither of which would have saved the crew from a

serious attack. A soldier basically found out if the attack had passed by taking off the gas mask and seeing whether he survived.

Above the crew was a canvas hood held in place by two tubular-section bows, this arrangement replacing the single bow on the MA to provide slightly more headroom without increasing the height of the silhouette. When the crew became tired of the sound of flapping canvas they could stow the bows flat, clamped to the sides of the vehicle, while the canvas itself could be stashed away under the front passenger seat.

Beside the driver's seat, on the outside of the Jeep, a shovel and axe were added to the MB. The 2.5kg axe and Number 2 spade were usually painted the same colour as the vehicle and were called into frequent use, just like the handles that were added to either side to enable the Jeep to be dragged out of ditches.

'Buckingham Palace, madam?' Willys MB 'slat grill' in London shows the windscreen folded flat, resting on the bonnet blocks.

Other changes from MA to MB (and hence to the GPW) included carrying the steering tie rods higher above the axles to keep them away from damage, sealing the spring shackles to keep water and mud out of them, protecting the hydraulic brake hoses, and standardising the black-out lights. A final change was to set the whole vehicle rolling on 6.00-16 tyres and Kelsey-Hayes split-rim combat wheels. These allowed the vehicle to run with a flat tyre for a while – an obvious advantage when under fire or you needed to get back to base before the mess shut. These rims ran non-directional tread (NDT) tyres from a variety of manufacturers, including Firestone and Goodyear. Of six-ply construction, the heavy-duty tyres ran inner tubes at 30psi.

Ford was determined to use its own components on the GPW as far as possible, but this plan did not work out too well. The Dearborn plant churned out 6.00-16 NDT tyres until the American government bought the entire tyre and tube facility in December 1942. As part of a deal with the Soviet Union, the whole plant was then shipped to Russia to help with their war effort. But, as far as can be ascertained, the plant was never actually reassembled and never went into production. An irritated Ford company then had to buy tyres from Firestone for the rest of the war.

It may seem normal to Americans or to modern readers, but the list of spares and accessories that went with each vehicle was really quite remarkable. This was a utility vehicle with a presumed short life span, yet each Jeep left the factory with a huge array of bits and pieces that split into two distinct groups. The first was the contents of the spare parts bag. This was a pretty standard list of emergency equipment like a spark plug, bulbs, cotter pins, fan belt, valve cores, tyre, inner tube and wheel. Alongside these spares was a comprehensive list of what were known as accessories. This small mountain of equipment included a huge tool kit, including a 16oz ball-peen hammer and a selection of wrenches (including

The compartment was not added until later Willys MB models – this is an early MB with manufacturer's plates on the bulkhead but no box.

Three plates on the lid of the passenger's stowage box (top), and the compartment itself complete with period kit (above).

a large adjustable one) and screwdrivers. Then there was a fire extinguisher, lubricating gun, two padlocks, tyre pump, jack, tyre chains and even a half-pound roll of electrical tape. Although there was a starter motor, a starter crank was included, stowed behind the rear seat. Both Willys and Ford included all the spares and accessories with every vehicle, although Ford mostly used tools bearing its own logo.

All these additions and changes added pounds and inches to the Jeep. On its own the change to combat wheels and associated tyres added 60lb to the weight. The final officially accepted weight for the MB had been 2450lb, but by the end of the war Jeeps were coming off the line over 100lb heavier. The MB was also 2in longer than its predecessor, measuring 132.75ins. It was now set

Canvas top in place, shovel and axe safely strapped on – this is what **hundreds of thousands of Willys and Ford Jeeps looked like.**

with an 80in wheelbase, 62in width and height to the top of the windscreen of just 63in. Within these overall dimensions lurked thousands of parts that came from many different suppliers, who, in turn, had to change what they provided according to the dictates of wartime procurement.

Many of the differences obviously originated in the fact that two companies were making what was ostensibly the same vehicle. However, as we have already seen, Ford in particular tried to put its mark, usually literally, on Jeeps coming out of its own plants. There are some weird anomalies, such as the rare combination of Ford GPWs which came off the line with Willys frames under them. These frames, made for Willys by the A.O.Smith Company, featured a tubular front cross member,

whereas the Ford version had an inverted U shape. It is probable that these frames were poured into the Ford system at an early point when Ford's production demands exceeded supply from its own sources.

Ford itself made Jeeps at several plants scattered throughout the USA, and from an early stage stamped its oval logo into the rear body panel. After about April 1942, however, this practice stopped to be replaced by the letter F, in several styles, most fairly florid. As the war neared its conclusion this practice also declined, but at one point just about every conceivable component carried the F letter somewhere on it. This extended to such minor items as locking washers and grease seals. About the only parts that didn't have an F on them were the valve cores, grommets, switches and gauges. It is not exactly clear as to why Ford went to the effort of all this marking but it may have had something to do with warranty work.

In 1943, with production running flat-out in every
available factory owned by either Ford or Willys, there
was a study to check that the two vehicles really were the
same thing. A GPW and an MB were stripped and
compared item by item. Given that the Ford was based
on Willys blueprints, it is unsurprising that no major
discrepancies were found, but some anomalies did come
to light after several weeks of checking. The Ford bonnet
was not as rigid as that of the MB, for example, and the
sliding gear on the Willys transfer case output would not
fit on the spline of the Ford transfer case output shaft.
Since these gears were a selected fit this did not matter
too much, but the supplier, the Warner Gear Company,
corrected the Willys output shaft, which was being made
fractionally too large.

Other differences were tiny, and a consequence of
slight changes between the Willys blueprints and Ford's
production methods. Obviously, these were only of
interest if they affected interchangeability of parts in the

**End of the line at a Ford
production plant (above).
The finished Jeep was
perhaps spartan inside
but came fully equipped**
**with kit. Note the Ford
name (below) stamped
into the rear panel of
this GPW, under the
jerrycan.**

Jeeps had a hard time in every theatre of war, but did not fail. This battered vehicle in service with the 25th Marine Division **has a long air inlet pipe attached to the carburettor through a hole in the bonnet – part of the Deep Fording Kit.**

field, so it did not matter too much that, for example, the diameters of the radiator bracket holes on the front frame cross member were ⅛in too small on the Ford.

What did emerge, although nothing seems to have been made of this at the time, were a couple of indicators that the life expectancy of the Ford-built engine was not going to be quite as good as the original Willys design. First, the Ford engine weighed 547lb, complete with transfer case, carburettor, electrics and starter, but without any oil – the Willys engine was 10lb heavier in the same condition. Second, and more worrying, was that the dipstick on the Ford-built engine was found to be set ⅜in too low, thereby giving the impression that the

engine contained more oil than was actually the case. As a result Ford engine blocks are rarer now than Willys versions, and longevity was not helped, in addition, by a change in casting design that meant the company turned out sub-standard engines for the last six weeks of 1944.

Production of the Ford GPW and Willys MB continued throughout the war, but naturally some changes were made as experience in combat filtered back to the factories. Some we have already seen, but others were still being made in the summer of 1944. The spare wheel, for example, caused problems as it was a heavy object suspended off the rear body panel. In October 1942 the panel was reinforced because vibration of the spare wheel bracket was causing breakages, but this still was not perfect and in August 1943 support was added under the wheel to try to brace the weight some more. You can imagine the minor problems that occurred in service when you learn of other changes, such as the adoption of heavy-duty chassis springs in June 1944, and

Ford was fanatical about leaving its mark on the GPW, although the full name stamp was replaced by a variety of florid F logos, albeit rather crudely done.

A restored panel with the full Ford logo prominently displayed.

the addition of a gusset to the rear of the frame to prevent cracking just a month later. You can grasp the heavy use that the Jeeps were subjected to by these and other changes, which were made around the time of the Normandy invasions on D-Day.

Extended, heavy use in every theatre of war, from desert to deep jungle, by troops who were tired, under fire and mechanically unsympathetic, with service intervals stretched even further than optimism and fatigue would ask for – these are the sorts of conditions when everything fails. Yet the Jeep did not fail. Certainly there were changes to bolts, wheels, seats and spring rates, but there was not a single major failure in the design throughout the war. No going back to the drawing board – everything had been right first time.

When you consider the gestation period of the Jeep

MAX SPEED
40 MPH

CAUTION
LEFT HAND
DRIVE
NO SIGNAL

The spare wheel weighed a lot and could cause fractures if the Jeep was smashed about the **countryside. Various remedies helped strengthen its support over the production run.**

this fact is truly incredible, an achievement that seems even more extraordinary when you compare it to modern military weapons systems and vehicles that

instantly become scandals the first time they go into combat, despite the computer hours and enormous budgets spent on their development.

The Jeep was one of those vehicles that changed the way wars were fought, and it remains one of the most extreme examples of how two competing companies, Willys-Overland and Ford, combined to demonstrate the mighty muscle of American industry in a time of crisis.

JEEP VARIATIONS

It is impossible to say exactly how many Jeeps were made, but the figure is substantially over 600,000, with many more assembled from special materials and sub-assemblies. They served in every theatre of war but then so did, for example, the Dakota. What was so remarkable about the Jeep was not so much that it could handle itself in the sort of terrain that gave camels, donkeys and porters pause for thought, but that it could adapt itself so perfectly to both location and function. If you applied Darwinian selection to the Jeep it would certainly come out as a survivor.

Although a standard Jeep was hardly the most comfortable means of transport, it could make a pretty reasonable mobile home. You could drive in it all day,

This is what desperate and ingenious troops could turn a Jeep into, in cold combat conditions. The front upright bar was to cut wires across the road, the extra doors kept some of the cold out, while the rear basket augmented the carrying capacity. The wheels carry mud floatation adapters invented by the imaginative Captain Rainhart of the 981st Engineer Maintenance Company in XII Corps.

and towards the end of the day put some food tins in the engine compartment. By the time you had stopped and camped up the food would be hot, then you could draw off some of the piping hot water from the cooling jacket and have a good wash before setting out a card game on

Major General Surtees inspects Belgian SAS units. Note the assorted machine guns and armour plate, as well as the unusual placing of the spare wheel in front of the radiator.

A simple conversion used the rotational speed of a wheel to turn a saw, which cuts wood for an Allied field hospital behind the 5th Army in Italy in 1944.

that sensibly flat front bonnet. As the famous war correspondent Ernie Pyle remarked: 'It's as faithful as a dog, as strong as a mule and as agile as a goat.' No wonder the GIs loved it.

But it was not the Americans who first used the most quintessential American vehicle in combat. Pearl Harbour had been bombed around the time the first Jeeps came off the line, but by then Germany had blitzed through Europe up to the English Channel and had then launched the assault on Russia. At the time, Congress was reluctant to become involved, but President Franklin D. Roosevelt managed to side-step the issue by starting Lend-Lease, whereby 'material resources' could be sent to foreign countries. At the end of the war the goods would be returned and reciprocal deals would be struck with the countries concerned. In other words, this was foreign aid.

Jeeps were among the first items to be sent to both Britain and Russia. A total of 5000 Jeeps went to Stalin, who appreciated their worth over the motorcycle and sidecar combinations originally asked for. The British, too, made good use of their Jeeps, particularly with David Stirling in the North African desert. The founder

Conversions to Jeeps included a third axle and even a half-tracked rear to increase mobility and the payload – usually weapons – that the vehicle could carry. Note longer wheelbase.

of the SAS used them for both reconnaissance and attack, painting them desert pink and loading them with machine guns and enough supplies for long-range patrols that lasted weeks.

With initial forays into the depths of the Russian winter and the Sahara Desert, the stage was set for the Jeep to emerge as one of the most versatile vehicles ever made. With minimal alterations, often carried out in the field, the Jeep could become everything from a freight train to an ambulance or a gun platform, and much more besides.

Train

Perhaps one of the most startling transformations was to convert a Jeep into a train. All you had to do was change the wheels for flanged steel rims and add a suitable

Just a couple of months after D-Day, the Railway Construction Company of the British Royal Engineers used this Jeep on the Caen-Cherbourg railway line in northern France, running patrols to check for cut wires, sabotaged rails and other enemy activity.

In the Far East, Jeeps were used not just to patrol railway lines, but also to pull the trains. At least they ran on time.

Ambulance and communications Jeeps struggle through the flooded streets of Cranenburg (above), just inside Germany in February 1945. Note the stretchers on the roof and the home-made covered sides. Australians with an ambulance in the Far East (left). Note how high the patients are carried, which could prove bad for their health with the enemy around. Snow chains for the tyres were equally effective in thick mud or snow.

coupling off the rear panel and there you were – assuming you had carried out the simple operation of locking the steering.

In Europe Jeeps ran along the main railway lines, pulling all sorts of goods behind them and checking the many miles of unprotected communication wires that ran beside the tracks, while in Australia they were used as switch engines. Even the Supreme Allied Commander, Lord Mountbatten, was transported in Burma in 1944 in a Jeep running on the railway between Mogaung and Sahman. But perhaps the finest effort was demonstrated in the Philippines, where a Jeep – with only a quarter-

ton chassis remember – pulled a 52-ton supply train for 19 miles, averaging 22mph. Even so, this probably was not what war correspondent Ernie Pyle had in mind when he called the Jeep 'a divine instrument of military locomotion'.

Ambulance

Jeeps could get troops up to the front line better than any other vehicle, but they also proved best for getting wounded men back again. Field modifications were carried out all over the world so that injured soldiers

An early Ford GP on manoeuvres in Louisiana in September 1941. D Company, 69th Division look happy with the centrally mounted .50-cal machine gun – so they should.

Serious firepower. An SAS Jeep in North Africa displays a formidable array of both single and twin Vickers K guns as well as a .50-cal machine gun liberated from an aircraft. To keep the crew in the field, there are 20 jerrycans plus sufficient supplies. This vehicle was destroyed by enemy aircraft and the crew had to start a 100-mile walk to safety.

could be carried on stretchers mounted on the Jeeps.

Normally this would entail nothing more than bolting or welding a frame extension off the rear body so that two stretchers would fit across the back of the vehicle, with possibly another stretcher going lengthways along the passenger side of the bonnet. Obviously the level of conversion depended on the skills, time and materials available and, at best, the ride must have been fast but uncomfortable. But some conversions featured canvas covers to stop the wounded being bounced out, and even sprung bases to the stretcher supports. More elaborate ideas included carrying up to five stretchers, but that could not be done without raising the silhouette dangerously high. Early efforts were simply metal frames that allowed two stretchers to be carried lengthways above the height of the windscreen. While this must have given the wounded a splendid view of the passing scenery, it also left them vulnerable to becoming even more wounded. The best modifications used the low silhouette of the Jeep to everyone's advantage. Nobody had a comfortable ride out of the combat zone, but at least they could get out, lying down, in reasonable time. The Jeep got them in, the Jeep got them out.

Gun platform.....................................

One of the useful design features of the Jeep was its plethora of flat surfaces and strong metal plate. With so little in the way of accessories on it – no cup-holders,

Jeeps of the US 7th Army in the fighting for Alsace were fitted with these 4.5in rocket launchers, taken from landing craft used for the D-Day invasion. The dozen rockets could be fired every 2sec, with metal plates to protect the vehicle from the back-blast.

The founder of the SAS, Lt Col Stirling, chats to an SAS Jeep crew – Cpl Kennedy (left, Royal Scots Greys) and Lt McDonald (DCM Cameron Highlanders), after a raid in 1943. Judging by the facial hair, they had been out in the desert for some time.

satellite navigation systems or automatic seat belt tensioners for starters – there was plenty of space to mount the little essentials of wartime existence, like guns. The Jeep was a nimble beast, but often running either forwards or backwards was not an option and then you wanted firepower. Early versions had a .50-cal machine gun mounted on a monopod behind the front seats. Soon, mounts were sprouting all over, often on the same vehicle. Mounts appeared on the passenger side instrument panel, in the centre of the vehicle and off the rear body. These would carry everything from Browning automatic rifles up through .30-cal and then .50-cal machine guns.

The big .50-cal guns were sometimes equipped with the long barrels and presented a fearsome appearance. Equally, they were awkward to fire, particularly at close quarters, as they took up so much room inside the vehicle. These big boys would normally be pedestal-mounted near the centre of the vehicle, which meant that the gunner had to stand off the rear of the Jeep or even outside it to take aim. Experience gradually led to the mounts being shortened, which decreased their area of operation but increased the life expectancy of the gunner. Despite these guns firing huge quantities of

heavy ammunition, the Jeep could take it, the tough suspension working in its favour.

Out in the desert, and then working their way into Europe, the SAS Jeeps tended to carry twin Vickers K303 or Bren machine guns on a mount in front of the passenger, with possibly another Bren mounted off the driver's side if he had a moment to spare. During 1941

Both Sgt Schofield and Trooper Jeavons had fought in the desert, so they were quite used to heavily armoured Jeeps. The two are seen in their Jeep of the 1st SAS Regiment in north-western Europe in 1944, with metal plate and armoured glass to protect them, should the primary protection of three machine guns fail.

and 1942 the SAS was refined under David Stirling to work alongside the Long Range Desert Group, both groups using Jeeps. They would raid runways and depots, causing enormous loss of material and diverting enemy troops that could have been used at the front.

SAS Jeeps looked shambolic but were packed with practical kit. Often a coolant expansion tank would sit off the front of the radiator to help stop boiling in the desert, while the bonnets and rears would be packed with racks of jerrycans carrying petrol and water. Satchels of kit, including Lewes pencil bombs for inserting into aircraft fuel tanks, festooned any area not occupied by a scruffy and dangerous looking soldier. The vehicles bristled with weapons, sometimes with twin Vickers K machine guns mounted off the rear plate, another Vickers K off the driver's side and a massive .50-cal machine gun, which would originally have been found on an aircraft, swivelling ahead of the front passenger.

Later on in the war, in 1944, Jeeps were converted in both the Pacific theatre and in Europe to carry rocket launchers. In the Pacific the T45 conversion gave 14 rockets fixed to the sides of the Jeep and was used by the US Marines. In Europe, mostly in the fighting around Alsace, two rows of six launchers were fired facing

forward, with the windscreen and front compartment protected from the back-blast by metal plating. These 4.5in launchers were similar to the ones used on the landing craft during the Normandy landings, and could fire rockets every two seconds. By the final year of the war there were even experiments with T19 105mm recoilless guns mounted in the middle of the vehicle. Given the speed of operation and the instant firepower that could be brought to bear, the Jeep could present a formidably hard-hitting and fast-moving target.

It could also tow a fair amount of firepower behind it. The favourite was the 37mm anti-tank gun, which could punch through light tank armour. This again extended the operational capabilities of the Jeep way beyond those of a simple four-seater communication and transport vehicle.

Protection

To further bolster their chances, a few Jeeps added protection in the form of body armour. As early as 1941 the Smart Safety Engineering Corp of Detroit had developed fully armoured Jeeps, although the weight penalty could be over 1000lb, but in the field some units

The Jeep made a highly mobile and versatile command vehicle and communications post. Here, Major General T.W. Rees, GOC 19th Indian Division, directs operations from his Jeep during the advance on Mandalay.

added metal plate in front of the radiator and in place of the windscreen.

Perhaps the only other major conversion, carried out mainly after the D-Day landings, was a simple one to protect the crew. It was added to most Jeeps in the European theatre after 1944, when the Germans developed the unpleasant habit of stringing wire across the roads at head height. Motorcycle despatch riders and the occupants of Jeeps formed most of the casualties that ensued. The answer was to weld an upright angle-iron pole to the front bumper, often braced by a couple of cross members to hold it in place if the pole hit a wire at speed. Like everything else, it did not take long before this anti-decapitation device was being refined, with the top angled forward and sometimes even notches cut into the pole to help trap the wire and cut it. It was one of the simplest, cheapest and easiest conversions carried out on the Jeep, but also one of the most effective.

Communications

The Jeep was not actually designed to replace a tank, as one of its main criteria was to act as a communications vehicle, either by moving messengers around or by receiving and transmitting radio signals. Radio use was built into Jeeps from the start, as even the earliest models off the line were fitted with radio suppression equipment.

Among the earth straps and suppression devices, the filterette was the largest component. This heavy box was bolted to the passenger side of the toe board, under the dash. It contained a coaxial capacitor to filter out interference, although this in itself was replaced by a series of smaller filters in the system at the end of 1943. At the same time a lot of grounding straps were discarded as being unnecessary. Some months before this some vehicles had their 6-volt electrics converted to 12-volt operation as radio vehicles, complementing the high-capacity generator and voltage regulator fitted.

Suitably equipped, these Jeeps carried out any communications task – acting as relays between units, operating as commanders' vehicles for directing operations, liaising between air and ground units to locate targets and direct aircraft to them. Usually this required so much radio equipment that the rear bench seat was replaced with kit, sometimes with a trailer-full being towed behind. The huge aerial, mounted off the rear of the driver's side of the vehicle, could either be left flying or tethered, via wires, looped up and over the front bonnet when not in use. Used with a reasonable supply of rations, the Jeep could thus become a mobile command post for long periods, which was particularly welcome in the intense island-hopping campaigns in the Pacific. But, then, the Jeep was always welcome.

Weather protection

If used as a command post in the European theatre, one of the more unwelcome aspects of living with a Jeep was

Happier times. The radio aerial could be tethered, as here, from the front of the Jeep when not in use.

The height of luxury, but not so good if you need to bail out in a hurry. Men of the 644th Ordnance Company of the US Army built this hot-house from salvaged aircraft parts. It even had a defroster.

merely exacerbated. The canvas weather equipment did not offer much protection, and in a European winter it was as good at keeping out the cold as it was at shrugging off artillery shells.

Trying to keep warm brought out the most ingenious solutions from depot crews and front-line units alike. Some simply added extra canvas to the sides, either in the shape of doors or just in long strips, but this would not seem such a good idea if you had to abandon the vehicle in a hurry. Many units, either at an individual or ordnance workshop level, would make a hard-top frame out of metal and then add sides of metal, wood or even Perspex. One particularly novel option used as a basis the cockpit from a B-17 bomber.

The British Army tried to do things on a more professional level and had Humber devise a system of side curtains and doors for the Jeep. American crews either just butched it out, preferably after 'borrowing' bomber crews' leather jackets, trousers and boots, or made up their own canopies, sometimes in a very homely way complete with wooden doors with handles taken from a house.

A British ATS girl fills up a Seep. The ability to fight on land or water regardless is a military dream, but it was not realised in the Seep.

Since the stock vehicle had no defroster and no heater, extra protection could prove essential, particularly in the fierce winter of 1944. But obviously it was not beyond the wit of many to rig up a heater to feed the front seats or a defroster for the windscreen, using a bypass from the engine cooling system. The extent of the conversions tended to depend on the rank of the freezing person, the time available and the level of inducement.

The Seep ....

It sounded like the best of both worlds – a Jeep that could also become a boat without doing anything other than flick a lever. Like so many ideas that are rushed into production, it did not work out quite that way.

The idea of a troop carrier and reconnaissance vehicle that could travel at up to 60mph on land but which could then cross rivers – particularly useful where bridges had

A Seep on US Army manoeuvres (top). The front spray deck and part sidescreens would help the crew a little. The wheels appear to be turning as well as the propeller, for extra propulsion. Free French soldiers (above) drive through a ruined Italian village in their Seep.

been blown and roads destroyed – was a good one. The problem was that there was little time to test the development vehicle fully. In 1942, Pearl Harbour having already been attacked, Marmon-Herrington, of whom we heard earlier, joined up with the boat-building firm of Sparkman and Stephens to develop a water-borne Jeep based on a Ford GPW. This was going to be a GP-A (General Purpose – Amphibious). What it became was the Seep (sea-going Jeep).

Bizarre though it seems, the design research for the Seep was done without a single Jeep being present, using only the statistics of a GPW that understated its weight by about 30%. The result was a hull that had far too little freeboard and was under-powered. Despite this, and only limited testing, the Seep was pushed into production by Ford in September 1942. By the following June production was stopped, after 12,778 had been built.

The Seep worked by a propeller at the stern driven by a shaft taken from the transfer box. This allowed propeller speeds to vary and also provided for a reverse gear. Steering was by way of a rudder aided by the front wheels, but otherwise the driver just controlled the

Unlike most Jeeps, this Seep will not get stuck when the tide comes in. Yet, unlike most Jeeps, the Seep was not a military success.

Private Jock Allingham turned his Jeep into a mobile and highly successful laundry.

Trying to manoeuvre and park bombers and fighters on crowded forward airfields could be confusing, so it was easier if the pilots had something they could focus on to follow.

The flat bonnet of the Jeep made it suitable for all sorts of purposes. This Anglican portable field altar fits perfectly – a game of cards could be accommodated just as easily.

vehicle as normal. Two levers by the transfer lever allowed him to bring in the propeller as he entered the water, and the bilge pump if water entered the Seep. The small dimensions did not allow sufficient buoyancy volume, while the extra 1336lb of weight kept the freeboard even smaller.

In operation the Seep did not work – but this was hardly surprising given that nobody seems to have asked the military whether it thought the vehicle sound in the first place. In Europe the rivers tend to run deep in the land, between steep banks or sometimes man–made walls. No amphibious vehicle can get out of a situation like this, although the gently sloping banks of the rivers in Russia were a different matter. Many of the Seeps went to Russia under Lend-Lease, and seem to have been reasonably effective in action on the Eastern Front. Perhaps the most appropriate epitaph to the Seep is that, after the war, Australian engineer Ben Carlin used a modified Seep to drive and float his way round the world – his vehicle was called 'Half Safe'.

The Jeep proved that it could do anything. Jeeps towed bombers, acted as 'Follow Me' vehicles on airfields for traffic control, became mobile bases for religious services, and used their power take-offs (PTOs) to run searchlights, radar, welders, cookers and even a laundry, while always keeping going to get men into battle and then get them out again. The Jeep answered whatever was asked of it.

DRIVING THE JEEP

American Congressmen inspect US Army equipment in October 1941. Note the obvious discomfort of the Congressman and the driver of this Ford GP. This is a good view of the fuel tank that the officer driver is sitting on.

The Jeep was a utility vehicle, built to be driven under all conditions by drivers with the mechanical sympathies of Barney Rubble. There was no point in adding unnecessary extras because they would simply be abused or broken.

Drivers could not even be trusted with a simple ignition key, so they were given the absolute bare minimum. Where a modern car has three mirrors, the Jeep had one. Instead of thick upholstery, Jeep seats had a couple of inches of hair and a few springs, even though normal use meant spine-jarring progress over potholed terrain. Instead of constant and intermittent wiper controls, there was a hand-operated handle. Almost every

MPs share a good joke. The .50-cal machine gun might cheer them up, but the need to give it a field of fire means nothing can be done to combat the cold.

Air Chief Marshal Tedder takes things into his own hands just after the Normandy landings in June 1944.

The lanky General Clark sprawls all over his Jeep while inspecting the troops at Anzio after the landings there in 1944.

other military vehicle had a solid roof, but the Jeep made do with some draughty canvas. Instead of heating and air conditioning, it had nothing to alleviate the temperature extremes of Russian winters and Saharan summers.

Captain Moon, writing in *Motor Sport* magazine about his experiences just after the end of World War II, commented that the canvas hood was 'apparently designed to provide as much draught as possible for the backs of all occupants' necks and to remind the driver when he is going too fast by flapping on the top of his head'. As we saw in the previous chapter, most occupants were forced to do something about the design when winter came – even a motorcyclist would have been warmer because he had special clothing. The Jeep earned its nickname of the 'Pneumonia Wagon'.

Life was more tolerable when the weather was warmer, but the basic design of the vehicle was not really suited to a comfortable ride. All those photos showing GIs and generals slouching in their seats, sometimes with their feet outside the vehicle, all look terribly atmospheric but they sat like that because they had to. The seats themselves really were not comfortable, so you either sat bolt upright, which was not sustainable, or else you slouched with your spine halfway down the seat.

Road legal and restored. Jeeps are still fun, but the ride causes this passenger to rely on an external grab handle to keep him in at speed.

Riding in a Jeep all day was never any pleasure.

The short wheelbase and fairly stiff suspension resulted in a choppy ride, and anyone who rides in a wartime Jeep nowadays will appreciate just how far suspension design on off-road vehicles has come in the last half century or so. Anyone who has travelled in one of the Jeep's highly sophisticated successors, the AM General Hummer, simply would not believe the difference. In the Hummer you sit under cover, even in the soft-top versions, with a heater and comfortable seats. The sheer width and length of the vehicle makes for an easier ride, but the sophisticated suspension takes an amazing amount of bumps out of even a fast drive. There is no doubt that the Hummer would get troops to battle in much greater comfort, and hence in a better condition to fight after a long ride, but it must cost proportionally an awful lot more than a Jeep did 50 years ago. And only time will tell if it lasts as long.

A closer look at World War II photos showing Jeeps carrying officers around – and an awful lot of officers

Field Marshal Montgomery looks snug in this Willys MB 'slat grill' (above), in spring 1942, but seems to be struggling to get comfortable in the back of another Jeep (right), while Winston Churchill soothes his discomfort with a cigar.

seemed to live in the things – reveals another telling point. The officers always sat in the front. They may have had a driver, but he always ended up sitting in the back if a couple of top brass were on board. The ride in front was hard but it was not as bad as the ride in the back, where you sat virtually over the rear axle and had much

less legroom. The back seat was justly notorious for giving the occupants piles, to the extent that the condition became known by medics as 'Jeep disease'.

During the intense winter fighting of the Battle of the Bulge, at a time when Germans were infiltrating behind

The German POWs in the back of this cattle truck seem to be enjoying the ride. Note the modifications like the ram's head on the grille, the windscreen cover and the odd tyres.

the lines dressed as Americans, there is a story that a Belgian sentry at a checkpoint stopped a Jeep and instantly arrested the three 'Americans', including a colonel, who were aboard. The sentry explained that he knew they were Germans because the aide was driving and the colonel was in the back. Rank has its privileges, and haemorrhoids were usually delegated to the rank and file.

One man who improved the situation for himself was the maverick General Patton. He tended to be driven around in a Jeep, so his post was the front passenger seat. You could recognise his Ford GPW by the two long brass horns on the bonnet but the real change was inside, where he had a large red leather seat installed.

Considering that the Jeep was designed with a low silhouette so as to be able to creep around a battlefield, it is surprising how loud the exhaust can be. This is not just a modern manifestation. Peter Garnier, writing in *Thoroughbred and Classic Cars* magazine, recalled that the Jeep 'made a positively terrible noise at speed on a tarmac surface, with the whine of its transmission, its very characteristic and unmistakable exhaust note, and the exceptional road noise set up by the cross-country combat tyres as fitted for use in Europe. There was, of course, no sound deadening whatever – anywhere'.

But it is not all bad. Many vehicles of this age are pretty cranky to drive, but the Jeep was designed to be user-friendly. Although the engine offers perfectly respectable power, it does not tie the chassis in knots.

Equally, it is not so under-powered that you have to thrash the valves off it to keep moving. Instead power comes in softly but steadily, from low down the rev range. Obviously a vehicle that only has three forward gears needs a reasonable amount of torque, and the 105lb ft available at a lowly 2000rpm is quite sufficient to stop the engine falling into a power hole between gears. Similarly, the 63bhp on tap at 3800rpm means that you can row the quarter-tonner along at quite reasonable road speeds.

Top speed is quoted as about 65mph, and a Jeep can cruise comfortably at around 50mph, even though it will be drinking petrol at a rate of around 15mpg. Acceleration is hardly going to worry drag racers but it can get from zero to 50mph in just under 19sec, which is not bad for a 50-year-old utility vehicle. To stir the gearbox up to get decent acceleration figures takes a light touch if you are to avoid graunching the gears, but a delicate feel to let the gears mesh together in their own time pays dividends. A Jeep is a rewarding vehicle to drive as it will repay finesse, although it also earned its reputation of being difficult for even the most lead-footed driver to break.

One of the surprises in driving a Jeep today is how smooth and mellow the four-cylinder engine remains. Bearing in mind that this is a tuned version of a car engine dating from the 1920s, its steady and really very pleasant character comes as a delight. 'Barney' Roos really did work magic on this block. It is hard to believe that this is just an old L-head, side-valve unit since it pulls

Discomfort takes on new meaning for these British troops testing a Jeep in the Middle East in 1942. Note the air intake held up by the nearest trooper. This test ended in a drowned Jeep and some waterlogged crew.

so steadily, even when measured against more modern overhead valve engines.

To complement the power delivery and gearbox, the steering is light and responsive – no power assistance of course – with what seems like a tiny turning circle. Actually, it is 38ft clockwise and 37ft anti-clockwise, which means you can turn round in a reasonably wide lane. That really would have been useful for a driver finding himself heading towards trouble fast, with nowhere to turn a normal vehicle before the bullets started whizzing past his ears.

There is no doubt, driving a Jeep now, that the ride is on the arthritic side. Those leaf springs may have been cheap to produce and easier to repair in the field than an independent suspension system, but they do subject the occupants to jerks and thumps, blows that are not really absorbed by the minimal seat padding. The short wheelbase can be felt on undulating roads as the vehicle rocks rapidly fore and aft, shaking the structure and occupants alike. Fully laden with four massive Texan GIs, plus all their kit, the ride quality would doubtless have improved a bit, but then it probably would not have been driven with the care that most Jeeps now receive.

Off-road in the mud this is less of a problem. Once in low ratio, which has a top speed of 33mph, but which hauls happily from tickover, the Jeep keeps on trickling along over really quite extreme terrain. Approach and departure angles are pretty good for what is quite a low-silhouette vehicle, and the short wheelbase does wonders for the ramp breakover angle – you are unlikely to belly

one out on its metal sump guard. Tyre design has moved along in the last 50 years, but the non-directional rubber still gives reasonable grip unless the mud becomes too glutinous. All in all, you can keep moving a long way off-road in a Jeep, certainly as far as some of the modern machines. But, unlike them, if you get stuck and there are a few of you aboard, you can simply grab hold of the handles and haul the Jeep onto harder ground. Do not attempt that with a Grand Cherokee...

The reason most modern off-roaders do not run rings round a Jeep is that they tend to be heavier, weighed down with more extras, bigger engines and bulkier components. The excellent power-to-weight ratio of the Jeep will enable it to skim over surfaces where other vehicles are starting to dig in, which of course is when they need all their extra kit. Naturally, modern machines do have some advantages, with longer suspension movement, better tyres, diff locks front, middle and rear, and even electronic traction control. They would get further than a Jeep but, if they got stuck, they are going to stay there and it is hardly a fair comparison. That is like comparing a Mercedes S-class with a Morris Minor.

A Land Rover would give a Jeep a good run for its money, but the Land Rover, of course, was first produced in 1948 and its design was strongly influenced by the Jeep. It is not the only one. Several vehicles from different continents, like the Mahindra from India and the Asia Motors Rocsta from Korea, are mainstream off-roaders based closely upon the original Jeep design. It

seems strange to be able to buy such things in the 1990s, but in terms of ride quality and go-anywhere ability, there is little difference between the current imitators and the original.

That is one reason why old Jeep rigs can still cut it on trail drives, particularly in rocky terrain such as that found in America. Over really big rocks, or 'slick rock' terrain, the Jeep's soft power is an advantage in letting the rubber get a decent grip, although in these conditions it might be wise to scrap the authentic tyres since they are not going to hang on against gravity as well as modern tyres. Equally, the Jeep's narrow width and short wheelbase mean that it can creep over boulder-strewn surfaces that might defeat a bigger 4×4, which could get stuck and suffer bent panels.

In such situations you need good all-round visibility, something that the Jeep provides even though some modern vehicles have a much higher viewing platform. It was designed so crews could scramble out in seconds at the first sight of an ME109 bearing down on them, and this facility now means that the driver is easily able to lean out of the side to check the route ahead. He or she will not have to do this all the time since the bonnet is

unusually low compared to many other off-roaders, so terrain can be assessed much closer than on similar vehicles. You can see the ground about 15ft in front of the driver's seat, but it helps if you run with the windscreen down or even off. The only major handicap is that transmissions tend to break through rock strikes and other shocks. The protective plating underneath is not really strong enough, so it is worth augmenting this.

Nick Jeffrey regularly trials this 1943 Ford GPW. It is reasonably standard apart from Firestone SAT tyres, a limited slip diff in the rear, raised compression and rear shock absorbers on the front to gain an extra inch of drop. It is a heap of fun to drive.

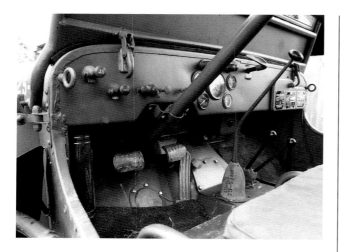

Note the starter switch, third control from left, installed after early **models were immobilised by the drivers wandering off with the keys.**

On the scrap heap. This sad pile of Jeeps and Seeps has been bulldozed **to the roadside during the hard-fought Rhine crossing in March 1945.**

The apparently unending agility and perseverance of the Jeep is its own downfall. At a time, 50 years ago, when ramp breakover angles were of less concern than the ability to get out of trouble fast, the last thing that was considered was whether a service was due. Naturally, many Jeeps were destroyed through enemy fire and mines, but many more were simply thrashed into the ground or crashed too badly to repair. There is a famous Bill Mauldin cartoon from the period where two GIs are rummaging through a pile of broken Jeeps until one says to the other: 'I'll be darned! Here's one wot wuz wrecked in combat'.

In mountainous terrain the Jeep could sometimes get where even mules could not, and of course they could be pushed on and on until they were irrevocably stuck. With mules you had to worry about cruelty and the fear that they might just lie down and die, but the Jeep would just keep on going and going – often to its own detriment. As one GI commented: "Lots of times a mule will balk if he doesn't think his leader is using good judgement. But a Jeep will always try".

Of course, Jeeps had the further advantage of not needing a fresh supply of oats, and you did not have to shout and wheedle at them to press on. But if there is one comparison to make about the relationship between soldiers and the Jeep, it would have to be that of a man and his horse. The gutsy, willing little quarter-tonner earned the love and respect of a lot of troops, whose lives were saved or enhanced by its presence.

However, anthropomorphism aside, there can be no doubt that the sheer volume of Jeeps around did colour the attitude of drivers to their vehicles. Despite the many stories, undoubtedly true, about how drivers cried when their Jeeps died, many a Jeep was horribly abused in the sure knowledge that if it broke then another would be there to take its place. After all, the US government's own assessment during the period was that a Jeep in a combat zone had a life expectancy of just 90 days.

JEEPS TODAY

In a rational world, there would be no Jeeps in existence. They were made cheaply and quickly, utility items to be used and thrown away or destroyed. We would now all be just reading about them and wondering how they compared to modern vehicles, while knowing full well that they belonged to a period past that had no relevance to modern living. With a life expectancy of just 90 days in combat no Jeeps should be left alive…

Of course not everyone wants the aggravation of owning a 50-year-old vehicle, but the desire is still there to at least be in touch with the 4×4 that started it all. That is one reason why Chrysler currently sells about half a million Jeep Wranglers in the USA every year and why the latest model features round headlights like the MB, rather than the square lamps found on the previous models. To some people, of course, that is like owning a replica, and dedicated fans must have the real thing.

More than half a century separates the 'slat grill' Willys MB from the 1997 Jeep TJ Wrangler, but the parentage is obvious, helped by the Wrangler reverting to small round headlamps.

By the end of World War II the US Army calculated that it had ten years' supply of new and unissued Jeeps stockpiled all over the country. That is a mouth-watering thought, but they soon started to be used up. As you can read in more detail in the next chapter, they were used in combat as well as for farming and utility purposes. None of these uses was considered 'soft', and the Jeep kept on working, and getting worn out, in its new roles. Many more were stored or abandoned by civilian and military alike. In America this was perhaps less critical due to the drier climate in many of the states, but vehicles in Europe soon fell prey to rust and decay.

For Sale: Jeep, project vehicle, nearly complete, needs some attention.

Nicely restored Ford GPW with radio mast. The owner spent years bringing this Jeep up to this level after finding it rusting in a hedge in England with seized engine and no head.

But many more were looked after, stored carefully or just used and maintained with care. The world still has a reasonable scattering of Jeeps around it, although most are obviously to be found in America. The extremes, perhaps, are best exemplified by somewhere like Egypt, where Jeeps are still uncovered from the sand having lain there virtually mummified since their use in the North African campaign of 1942, and England, where even now

Jeeps are discovered mouldering away being used as chicken coops, with rust having done a better job on the bodywork than an 88mm shell.

Wherever you are, some basic checks will help you ascertain what you are buying and whether it is worth the purchase. Quite a few CJ2As, which started coming off the production lines alongside the last of the MBs, have been tarted up to look like war-vintage machines,

An early 'slat grill' Willys MB, like this one, will **cost serious money if it is in this prime condition.**

but the rear tailgate is an instant giveaway. Not much else is going to pass for an MB or GPW unless the purchaser has blinded himself to the obvious.

The easiest route is to buy a fully restored and complete Jeep, but you can expect to pay serious money for such a rarity – and this kind of purchase will leave you with no scope to imprint your own work and knowledge onto it. The most difficult route is to buy a bag of bits and try to work it up from there, but you just know that not all the parts will be there, whatever the vendor claims. On the whole it works out better to buy the most complete Jeep you can find since, as with any type of vehicle, making one up from parts is both more expensive and more time-consuming.

Look carefully at what you are considering buying. What may at first look a wreck might not need as much work or money spent on it as one that, at first glance, seems smarter. The sheet metal of the bodywork is bound

to have some surface rust, but this is nowhere near as bad as full rust-through, which will mean repair or replacement. However, the bodywork is relatively easy and cheap to repair compared to the steel of the chassis.

The chassis, the basis of the vehicle, will have taken some massive strains in its life while being constantly bombarded with everything from rocks to mud. Some will have cracked or broken under the strain, and close examination may reveal welded-on brackets and plates where this has happened. Assuming you want the Jeep to look right, you are obviously going to have to tear down the whole vehicle and have the chassis rails repaired or replaced, a much more involved job than finding a new bonnet to bolt on.

Look carefully at places where components have been welded to the frame, like the shock absorber mounts, to check for rust or bad repair if they have broken away over time. Make sure, too, that nothing has been added to the chassis, since this will indicate that the vehicle has had to perform some other arduous task for which it was not designed, with consequent stress pouring through the

whole machine. Having said all that, a Jeep chassis is usually more rust-free than a comparable Land Rover one, for example, as there are few places to seal in water.

People tend to become very strung up about the engine, but it is only an engine and any engine can be repaired. Naturally it is preferable for an engine to be in working order or at least able to turn over, but repairing

Four-stage assembly sequence. First, the chassis has been repaired and painted, and the mechanicals rebuilt. Second, a new body is lowered into place on fabric shims that have **been glued between chassis and body. Third, the main tub in place, ready to be bolted down. Fourth, wings and bonnet are added quite simply, everything easily lifted by four men.**

it will usually be easier than sorting out a damaged chassis. As noted earlier, the Ford engines in the GPWs were perhaps not quite as reliable as the Willys versions, so you are less likely to find one in good working order.

This is not the place to describe fully how to dismantle and rebuild a complete Jeep, but there are some tips and advice that help to get one going and,

more importantly, keep it going. Given that most body panels are either flat or simple curves, repairing existing panels or making new ones should not be beyond most restorers. Go easy on the filler and instead panel-beat damage out after stripping off all signs of paint and rust.

Take an overview on the piece you are working on: it is too easy to repair the main damage on it at some

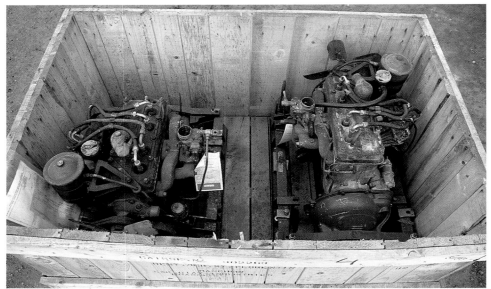

Attention to detail. This Ford GPW has been scrupulously worked on, complete with driver's manual in the zipped compartment (above left) of the cotton duck material seat. Note the notch in the dash (above) just above the handbrake lever – this is found on genuine bodies and some replicas.

Re-manufactured engines, crated while they await service and repair at RR Motor Services in England.

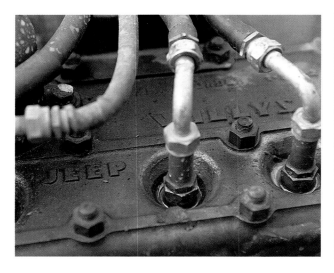

The stamping on the head (left) identifies this as a post-war engine, probably from Hotchkiss.

It may be French, but this engine (above) has been sent to an English specialist for repair.

This is a typically restored Jeep, in good working order, rather than a concours winner that never turns a wheel. The purist would not like the different tyres, just for starters.

effort only to realise that several other areas on the same panel also need fixing. Sometimes it will be easier to buy a new panel or make one yourself. Wooden formers, some 18-gauge steel and a MIG welder (which operates with less heat) are all you really need to make a panel that is as good as what the factory produced – after a bit of practice on something less critical first.

If you can find an original body, all well and good, but do not let the puritan in you totally ignore the fact that new parts are being made for the Jeep. Ever since the original stopped coming off the line, there have been parts made for the Jeep, either as the French Hotchkiss in the 1950s and '60s or later as replacement parts for vehicles that were obviously going to keep running for some time.

Many replacement Jeep parts of excellent quality nowadays come from the Philippines, and Taiwan is another source. The ultimate accolade is that some Jeep builders, who really know their stuff, specify Philippines-sourced parts over the original items as quality is higher. The Philippine company Genmark is often cited as one of the best, particularly for its bodies and panels. Spotting the difference between one of these new bodies and an original is not easy – except it will not be rusty – but there is one useful tell-tale. Original Jeep bodies have a small notch, about 1⅛in long by ¼in deep, in the middle of the fascia panel, possibly to take up flex in the panel as

This is a modern engine, nearly completed, built with virtually no original parts, finished in Ford colours. It will run very nicely, thank you.

it curves around the dash. Some of the later French-manufactured Hotchkiss bodies also have this notch, although it was omitted on early versions. Apart from the difficulty of determining a body's origins, from a standpoint of keeping the vehicle running, as opposed to polishing it, perhaps it does not do always to stick with 50-year-old stock that was made in a hurry and with wide tolerances in the first place. That is a personal and subjective choice open to every owner.

On any Jeep but the best, the engine is almost certainly going to need a complete rebuild – a simple oil change and service will not be enough. Working round the edges first, the fuel pump may well be tired, often brought about by the diaphragm becoming old and brittle, something that applies to new old-stock pumps. You will have to buy a more recent pump and take out the guts to fit the old item. The air cleaner, which uses oil to filter out dust, needs more regular servicing that a paper type, and water can accumulate and sit under the oil, rotting the body of the filter. The third filter, for the engine oil, was fairly inefficient at best and can easily

cause damage if it is not regularly cleaned and inspected. Regular oil and filter changes are essential preventative maintenance.

On the engine itself, a cracked block is not only far from unknown, but also one of the most serious problems. Often the problem is exacerbated by frost damage, so look for a block that has been drained rather than one just left lying around with old water in it, and have it carefully checked for cracks. Ford blocks were more vulnerable to damage than Willys ones, but finding replacement original blocks of either make is not easy.

Although it might make the purist wince, it could be said that fitting new items rather than new old-stock is the best way forward with the engine, as with other areas of the Jeep. Components like pistons, valves and gaskets are now being made to a higher quality than the original stock. Again, French engines are commonplace, often

Gold Beach, Normandy, 6 June 1994, half a century after D-Day. A Seep and assorted Jeeps try to hide the two Indian Jeep-based Mahindras.

with 'Willys' or 'Jeep' cast into the cylinder head, a feature that sets them apart from an original engine.

Newer blocks will often run the later gear-driven camshaft rather than the chain-driven wartime one, which is not quite as accurate. Along with this, you can fit a high-volume oil pump, such as the one made for the later CJ-5 model, which will help to keep your engine running longer and more quietly. Even though modern engine components build in something of a safety net, do not be tempted to go for much higher compression unless the engine has been seriously rebuilt. Marrying a high-compression head to a rather tired block will lead to yet another rebuild distressingly rapidly.

The gearbox has a pretty good record, but the synchromesh – fitted to second and third only, remember – is rather weak, and older 'boxes can have a tendency to jump out of second gear.

Water is once again the main enemy when it comes to the steering. It seeps past the horn button and trickles all the way down the steering tube to the steering sector housing. If the water freezes it will shatter this housing, but in any event it will almost certainly damage the bearings inside. Play in the steering linkage, almost inevitable after years of use and improper maintenance, will lead to characteristic front end shimmy, which needs fixing if you want to stay on the road or, if you are already off-road, stay the right way up.

Brakes also suffer from the ingress of water, which tends to be absorbed by cheap brake fluid and will destroy everything from brake lines to caliper pistons. Use top-grade silicon brake fluid after cleaning out the whole system.

Although you can still find, if you search hard, many parts still protected in their original greased paper wrappings, there are few areas of the Jeep that cannot be restored with new and high-quality replacements that generally look just the same. If you have casings for the gearbox, steering box and transfer box, along with a

Modern-day perfection. Everything neatly painted up, with the stencils placed accurately.

The wartime reality. Private Curtis of 8 Corps REME Workshop, in his green period. Taken in early 1945, it shows what really happened in the field.

chassis and axle casings, then you can build up the rest from replacement parts.

Determining the colour you paint this restored beauty is rather more complex than it should be, simply because nobody can really agree on the exact tone of 'olive drab'. Any existing paint has deteriorated over the years and cannot be used as a match, nor can memory or early colour film. Virtually all Jeeps were olive drab, apart from the grey ones used by the US Navy. Under the bonnet some items, like air filter, radiator and generator, were black, although on Ford GPWs the engine block, bellhousing and head were all grey.

The question of marking up a Jeep is similarly loose. You could go by the manuals and work out exactly how far from the bonnet edge the star should be placed, but in the field the task of marking up vehicles was often seen as a minor punishment and so was done with a distinct lack of enthusiasm and the artist's eye. Photos show troopers spraying paint all over the place and slopping on decals in a style reminiscent of the Deconstructionalists.

Above all, the work you do, the money you spend and the time you take should all be enjoyable. Anything that has kicked around this planet for half a century or more is not going to be exactly as it was and only a dedicated few would attempt to make it so. Driving a Jeep is one of life's pleasures and working on it should be

too, helped by the fact that it is simply designed and constructed, and you can get at just about any part without having to have a degree in electronics. You will be dealing with rusty metal and seized bolts, with a body tub that has been 'civilianised' by having a tailgate cut in, the canvas removed and the lights missing, with rotted seats and a crank that will not turn. Have fun.

THE JEEP'S POST-WAR EXISTENCE

For so many products and people, the end of World War II meant the end of their purpose, but not for the Jeep. Given the intensity and ferocity of the war, and the massive volumes of vehicles that were turned out, one could be forgiven for thinking that it took until the end of the war for people to start thinking about the peace. Not so at Willys-Overland.

As early as December 1943 Willys was considering the possible impact of so many ex-military Jeeps on the domestic car market at the close of hostilities. At this stage George W. Ritter, Vice President and General Counsel at Willys-Overland, responded to a request from

Taken just a few months before the end of the war, this photo is a reminder of just how many wrecked Jeeps there were all over the place, to be cannibalised or left to rot.

the Congressional Manasco Committee to examine ways to adapt the wartime vehicle for civilian use.

After studying the options Ritter recommended that the Jeep have a power take-off so that it could operate as a static power source or run ancillary equipment. Given that people were obviously contemplating agricultural use, he suggested gearing down both transmission and

THE SUN NEVER SETS ON THE FIGHTING JEEP

AVENGING JEEPS BLAST JAPS FROM CHINESE VILLAGE!

transfer case so that the Jeep could run steadily at low speeds – ploughing at 60mph would be exciting but short-lived. Along with that, the cooling system would have to be uprated to cope with constant work with low volumes of cooling air passing through the radiator. He also admitted that there would need to be a much better dealer network to sell and service these vehicles since Willys dealers were relatively few and far between.

While discussions and development work went on, so did the war and so did production of MBs at Willys and GPWs at Ford. On 7 May 1945 the war in Europe ended with Russian and American forces – both using Jeeps – meeting in Berlin. That still left the dreadful charnel houses of the Pacific as the Americans and the Allies closed in on Japan overland and island by island. The Jeep played an important role in the rapid movement of men, material and information, helping to bring about the final end to the war in the world on 14 August.

With peace came a whole new set of demands, not least the resumption of rivalries between motor companies that had worked together during the war. Ford, however, was not in the running for continuing

with production as the government had terminated its ninth and final contract with Ford on 15 August 1945. During the war Ford produced 277,896 Jeeps, according to its own figures, as well as Liberator bombers, M-10 tank destroyers, trucks, tugs and engines for both tanks and aircraft. The sheer volume of output achieved by Ford shows that the original decision to turn over blueprints to it, taken in the face of fierce opposition from Bantam, was the right one.

Post-war Ford had new programmes to work on instead of continuing to make a fighting vehicle to another company's blueprints, but Willys-Overland was determined to keep up the momentum established by the Jeep. The company's wartime motto had been 'The sun never sets on the Willys-built Jeep' and it was determined to live up to that claim.

It was obvious that the industrial fighting would only really start once military peace was restored, but Willys had found the time even during the war to start flexing its muscles over the defence of the Jeep. As early as 1942 Willys advertisements were planting the seed with comments like, 'Tomorrow, make your first new post-

74

The Sun Never Sets On the Mighty "Jeep"

JEEP-PLANNING!

"'Will she pull a plow?'... 'What's her draw-bar horse power?'... 'Bet she'd be great stuff on a hay loader or a hay hook'... 'Can she do 60 on the high-way?'... 'How about pulling a binder and running a separator?'... 'How about road grading and snow plowing?'... 'Will she buzz wood?'... 'Will she haul a corn picker and fill a silo?'"

Not only farmers but men in all walks of life and in all kinds of businesses are eyeing the amazing "Jeep", with postwar uses in mind.

On every battlefront and in every country touched by this war both soldiers and civilians link the names "Jeep" and *Willys* together. Are *you* Jeep-planning? Willys-Overland Motors, Inc., Toledo 1, Ohio.

★ ★ ★

A Michigan Farmer says:—

"From where I sit, the tough 'Jeep', with its great war record, has already set a standard for postwar transportation and work. This 'Jeep' is *new, modern*—the kind of equipment that can be made to serve both farm and city at work or at play. Willys has done an *historic* job."

Willys *Builds the Mighty* 'Jeep'

'The sun never sets on the Willys-built Jeep' is what it often said (facing page), in a side-swipe at

Ford. Winning the war was one thing (above), winning the peace quite another.

war car a Willys – The Jeep in Civvies'. Other ads of the period took a good swipe at Ford, which after all only made the vehicle to Willys specification, with a Willys engine: 'The heart of every fighting Jeep in the world – and the source of its amazing power, speed, flexibility, dependability and fuel economy – is the Willys 'Go-Devil' Engine, the design of which was perfected and is

owned exclusively by Willys-Overland'. Funny how the overall Bantam vehicle design does not get a mention...

During 1944 Willys built 22 prototypes of a civilian vehicle known as the CJ-1A (Civilian Jeep, first model of the Army). While the design of the MB stayed relatively locked, work on a post-war Jeep continued to the point where both MB and CJ models were on the production line together. On 12 July, a month before the end of the war with Japan, the CJ-2A was unveiled to the press by Charles Sorensen, Vice Chairman of Willys-Overland.

There was no mistaking the provenance. The major differences, apart from the lack of olive-drab paint, were an opening tailgate, which necessitated moving the spare wheel to the passenger side rear, 7in headlamps (instead of 5in), an automatic windscreen wiper and a fuel filler to the side instead of under the driver's seat. As George W. Ritter had suggested, gear ratios were altered, the cooling improved and the clutch strengthened. Importantly, for a model intended for people to buy and use, not be forced to sit in, the leaf springs were softened, the shock absorbers improved and the seats made more comfortable.

The CJ-2A was still very much a Jeep, looking pretty similar to the MB, and it was available for just $1090. For that you bought something that either you or your father could recognise from the war years, yet with civilian improvements. Under the bonnet 'Barney' Roos's Go-Devil engine still churned out the power, albeit with revised cylinder head, and the whole machine was as easy to service as the wartime MB. Given the lack of production time, to the extent that some companies, including Willys, had trouble getting car bodies made, and given the shortage of some materials like sheet steel, the CJ-2A was a practical solution to the post-war years. And, boy, was it practical.

Given that this was still a vehicle for driving to work

Put 'Jeep' Power to Work on Your Farm

IT SAVES YOU TIME... IT'S DEPENDABLE... THE 4-WHEEL-DRIVE

'UNIVERSAL'
Jeep
with Hydraulic Lift

TWO GREAT LINES OF 'JEEP' TRUCKS FOR THE FARM

SEE YOUR WILLYS-OVERLAND DEALER
WILLYS-OVERLAND MOTORS, Toledo, Ohio, MAKERS OF AMERICA'S MOST USEFUL VEHICLES

The agricultural purpose Willys-Overland envisaged for the Jeep, advertised in *Country Gentleman* in 1948, was well-proven.

Looking rather sorry for itself now, this late Willys MB has been 'civilianised' to resemble the CJ-2A more closely. Note the heater, electric wiper motor and the tailgate cut into the rear.

or taking the family shopping, it came with an amazing list of optional accessories from the Willys factory. While the war was still raging the Toledo factory was sending out advertisements that combined an MB with machine guns blazing behind a civilian Jeep down on the farm, and it was this agricultural life at which the CJ-2A was aimed. Several ploughs were on offer, alongside brush and bog harrows, a 6ft pasture cultivator, a similarly sized farm mower and a terracing blade. The rear power take-off was perfect for using a power-operated implement towed behind the vehicle.

This Universal Jeep could also come with weather protection, echoing the efforts of freezing troops who had come up with some ingenious solutions during the war. And inside there was a heater – what the troops would have given for that. Less useful for them would have been the King-Seeley governor, so that engine speeds could be set at 200rpm increments from 1000rpm

up to 2600rpm, making the Jeep more controllable for ploughing fields and other farm tasks. The Jeep was never going to replace the tractor but, until production of the CJ-2A ceased in 1949, it performed many of its functions around the farm, while using less petrol and proving endlessly reliable.

While the CJ-2A was selling well, of course, thousands of MBs were left without a job to do. In many ways the new version simply improved on the functions carried out by the wartime vehicle. While waiting for D-Day, American troops were photographed ploughing English fields with their Jeeps and using the long-suffering engine as a source for all manner of tasks. What GIs really felt about harrowing a flat, muddy field in the English rain was not dwelt upon...

Famously, Jeeps were used to lay cables at outlying airfields in Australia, with one Jeep pulling a plough to carve the trench, another laying the cable and a third rolling it all flat again, taking a tenth of the time and effort. The Jeep's practical application for peacetime use was not lost on anyone.

War-weary MBs were pressed into service throughout America, taking hunters and fishermen into

Indo-China saw many Jeeps getting back into action. This MB has been heavily armoured and armed with an automatic rifle.

Vietnam Light Infantry soldiers pose in their armoured Jeep with its .30-cal machine gun and driver protection with personal touch.

the wilderness, delivering mail, helping forest rangers and public utility workers, even harvesting citrus fruit in Florida. Fred Heine, a Kansas farmer, bought an ex-military Jeep as early as 1943 when it was being pensioned off, and paid $750 for it. Before this he used draught horses on his farm but, according to him, "they did nothing my Jeep can't do".

The Jeep as a practical working tool was an idea that worked out well. What did not work out was the hope that thousands of GIs, with fond memories of their Jeeps, would buy one at the end of the war. In fact the opposite happened, generally speaking, and they shied away from the ruthless practicality and discomfort. So too did their wives and girlfriends.

The Jeep was left to a life of hard work in civilian hands, endlessly ploughing fields, running compressors and generators, and being laden with more equipment than a train of mules. It was a far cry from the shot and shell, but the World War II Jeep did not end its service surrounded by chickens and cows.

By the time of the Korean War in the next decade, the MB had been replaced by the M38 and M38A1, both of which leaned heavily on their wartime predecessor in design. However, supplies being what they are, plenty of MBs continued to see action in Korea, and their usefulness did not stop there. Several armies, notably those of France and Israel, maintained strong fleets of

The enduring legend. This photo was taken in Morocco in 1958 and shows one of the early 'slat grill' Willys MBs with the French Army.

1940s-vintage Jeeps, running them wherever their influence or empire demanded.

With so many Jeeps having been produced, they ended up all over the world. Many of the Willys MAs, for example, went on Lend-Lease to Russia, while others stayed at home in American training camps. Those Soviet Jeeps were in use for many years all over the Russian empire. Similarly, French-sourced Jeeps turned up all over Africa and were serving with military units as far apart as the Ivory Coast and Algeria.

Peace-keeping forces, usually strapped for money, used Jeeps right up into the 1960s, so that both combatants and peace-keepers were using Willys MBs

This Jeep, still in active service, was recently photographed in Indonesia.

All over the world, they still work for a living. This Bushfire Unit Jeep is in Australia, not much modified.

and Ford GPWs in the various Arab-Israeli conflicts. In another twist, the Austrian Army, which during the war had been using its own versions of the Jeep like the *Schwimmwagen*, used both Willys and Ford Jeeps during the 1950s. These were even equipped with 106mm SR guns, which at that time were found on the later M38 model in the inventories of the Americans and Allies. An exception to this pattern, however, was Britain, where the Land Rover had taken over, having been based solidly on the Jeep design.

World War II, Korea, Vietnam, Algeria, Sinai –

wherever there was conflict you would find the Jeep, increasingly an elderly combatant, and increasingly weighed down with both years and equipment. But the Jeep was a machine of both war and peace. While desperate men around the world tried to kill or run from other men, often in Jeeps, others were peacefully harrowing their fields or delivering mail – also in Jeeps.

Whatever you wanted, it was. Whatever you asked, it provided. It was the mirror of our aspirations, and it carried out those aspirations with a degree of reliability and purpose that made it a legend.

APPENDIX

Production figures . . . .

FORD MOTOR COMPANY

Pygmy	2
GP	4458
GPW	277896
Total	**282356**

WILLYS-OVERLAND MOTORS INC

Quad	2
Model MA	1555
Model MB 'Slat Grill'	25808
Model MB	335531
Total	**362896**

AMERICAN BANTAM CAR CO

Prototype	1
MkII	69
Model 40-BRC	1175
Supplementary orders	1430
Total	**2675**

Total Jeep production	647927

Serial numbers and dates . . . .

WILLYS-OVERLAND MOTORS INC

MB 'Slat Grill'

100212 (first)	18 November 1941
125731 (last)	6 March 1942

MB

127130 (first)	12 June 1942
459824 (last)	21 September 1945

FORD MOTOR COMPANY

GPW

500 (first)	13 February 1942
277367 (last)	23 July 1945

Note Output varied dramatically: Ford GPW production, for example, ranged from just 77 units in January 1942 to 10,762 in June 1942.

Technical specifications . . . .

WILLYS MB/FORD GPW

Engine Go-Devil in-line four-cylinder **Construction** Cast iron block, cast iron L-head cylinder head, forged steel connecting rods, aluminium alloy three-ring pistons **Crankshaft** Three main bearings **Bore × stroke** 3.125in × 4.375in (79.4mm × 111.1mm) **Capacity** 134.2cu in (2199cc) **Valves** Single chain-driven camshaft, pushrod-operated side valves **Compression ratio** 6.48:1 **Fuel system** Carter single-barrel down-draught carburettor **Maximum power** 60bhp at 3600rpm **Maximum torque** 105lb ft at 2000rpm **Transmission** Warner Model T-84-J three-speed gearbox (synchromesh on second and third), Borg & Beck 7.875in (200mm) single-plate dry clutch, two-speed transfer case with two- or four-wheel drive **Gear ratios** First 2.67:1, second 1.56:1, third 1.00:1, reverse 3.55:1 **Axles** Spicer fully floating, hypoid bevel **Chassis/body** Steel frame with two box-section side rails and five cross-members, steel body bolted at 16 points **Suspension** Aluminium alloy leaf springs (eight leaves front, nine rear), Bendix hydraulic shock absorbers **Brakes** Bendix twin-shoe drums, Lockheed hydraulic actuation **Steering** Variable ratio (12-14:1) Ross cam and twin lever **Wheels/tyres** Split-rim 6.00×16in wheels, six-ply NDT tyres **Length** 122in (3350mm) **Width** 62in (1600mm) **Height** 69in (1750mm) with top raised **Wheelbase** 80in (2030mm) **Gross weight** 3243lb (1471kg) **Payload** 800lb (363kg) **Approach angle** 45 degrees **Departure angle** 35 degrees **Fording depth** 18in (45.7cm) **Fuel capacity** 15 US gallons (12.5 Imperial gallons, 56.7 litres) **Maximum speed** 65mph **0-50mph** 19sec

Ford GPW communications Jeep at 'snail mail' outpost.

ACKNOWLEDGEMENTS

Grateful thanks are due to everyone who provided illustrations and assistance during the preparation of this book. Specially commissioned photography by Morris Carpenter features Jeeps owned by Richard Gadeselli and Nick Jeffrey. Other photos were provided by Gary Stuart, John Carroll, Bart Vanderveen, the Imperial War Museum (thanks to Paul Kemp and David Hodges), Ford Motor Company, the National Automotive History Collection in Detroit (thanks to Serena Gomèz, Mark Patrick and Tom Sherry), *Classic Cars* magazine (thanks to Maurice Rowe), *Classic and Sportscar* magazine (thanks to Ed Herridge), Margus Kuuse and Nick Baldwin. The assistance of Tim Fuggle of RR Motor Services of Bethersden, Kent, was also invaluable.